Dear Reader,

Lake Constance, the Allgäu, mountains, the Ries, gently undulating hills and the idyllic Donauried – what a multi-faceted landscape! In addition, a colourful kaleidoscope of architectural highlights: magnificent monasteries, majestic castles (and not only the ones built by »Mad King Ludwig«), episcopal residences, and former free imperial cities still steeped in history. Bavarian Swabia is more than just a holiday region. Anyone who lives in this paradise of a landscape would scarcely be amazed that the north-south span of Bavarian Swabia corresponds precisely to that of the Holy Land, because he knows he lives in the Promised Land already. The people here are down-to-earth, calmly self-confident, interested, and open to new developments while being securely rooted in centuries-old tradition.

The region is anything but provincial. This book presents the stunning and spectacular as well as the silent, subtle beauties of Bavarian Swabia, and in so doing becomes a magnificent kaleidoscope of landscape, history and culture, of traditions, churches and monasteries, and of people and their destinies. Seventeen clearly laid-out, richly illustrated chapters invite you on a voyage of discovery, making you curious about sights both familiar and less well-known (because one of the main traits of the local inhabitants is a reluctance to brag about their best-kept secrets). For tourists this is more than a travel guide, for locals it is a stimulus to rediscover their native region – and possibly even the regions that lie beyond it.

Some of our authors were born in the region, others moved there (and are thus known as Neigschmeckta) but all of them are not only connoisseurs and insiders but also great lovers of Bavarian Swabia, this historical patchwork of different areas. The articles reflect the full spectrum of different mentalities among the local population: their Swabian sobriety, their typical understatement that hides a very secret pride in what generations of forebears have created, their fondness for witticisms and sometimes for a good old-fashioned argument, their great attention to detail, but above all, their happy and relaxed »live and let live« attitude to life. The cunning edge that the Swabians have inherited from their farming forebears goes hand in hand with a cosmopolitan attitude, their stolid bourgeois ways contrast with a tolerance born of their history, and their awareness of tradition is often countered by a critical openness with regard to progress. All of which makes this peaceful region of Germany, with its beautiful sights, all the more appealing.

This book reflects the endearing aspect of Bavarian Swabia. In the long process of its creation, in discussions with authors and employees – whom the publisher would like to thank heartily now that the work is over – this endearing side of Bavarian Swabia has been captured in texts and photographs. What at first seemed a rather risky undertaking – portraying the heterogeneous variety of Swabia from Lindau to Oettingen and Füssen to Weissenhorn in a mere book – turned into an exciting expedition with numerous discoveries, for me as well as everyone else involved in the project. If you happen to live in Swabia, I hope that rediscovering your region from several rather unusual angles will be as much fun for you as was for me. If you are visiting this marvellous region and are looking for more than just the usual »tourist information«, this book will give you numerous insights into the sheer variety offered by Bavarian Swabia. And who knows – it may even become your »Promised Land«, too!

Warmest regards,

Harald Hollo

Harald Hollo

Contents

ISBN 3-935438-01-X

Near Altusried, the river Iller cut through the boulders and loose rock of the terminal moraine and entered Tertiary sands. Farms dotted across the green slopes are a distinctive feature of this landscape.

NATURAL REGION AND CULTURAL LANDSCAPE

Swabia is often likened to the kind of colourful patchwork rug produced by the local weavers. This is not only because of the sheer variety of regions owned by princes, counts, monasteries and knights that determined the political situation here for centuries, but also because of the numerous different landscapes and stretches of natural scenery that are such a distinctive feature of this area of Germany, which is bounded geographically by the Iller and Lech rivers, the Ries and Lake Constance.

The interrelationships and affinities between nature and culture cannot be overlooked. »Just as the ecologist cannot ignore a snail-shell when researching into the life of the snail, human society and its historical development can never be properly understood if it is not seen in the context of its landscape.« This geographical insight also holds true for Swabia.

Relief, geology, climate, soil and vegetation have all had a decisive influence on the extent and amount of settlement, farming, house construction, trade, and on the growth of villages and towns. The aims and requirements placed on a natural region by its inhabitants are not only agricultural but also political and industrial, and depend greatly on technological potential, too.

The interrelationship of nature, man, space and time has created a complex system of cultural landscapes in which farms, meadows, villages, towns, castles and monasteries are just as important as streets, shopping centres or sports facilities.

Each cultural landscape is an archive of industrial development as well as a storehouse of the cultural achievements of numerous generations throughout the centuries.

A view across the eastern part of the Ries basin, showing the eastern crater edge between Oettingen and Ronheim. At the centre is the table-mountain-like shape of the Rollenberg, in the foreground the houses of Großsorheim and the intensively used agrarian landscape (Photo: H. Schmidt-Kaler in »Meteoriten-krater Nördlinger Ries«, by kind permission of the Dr. Friedrich Pfeil publishing house, Munich).

The Landscapes of Swabia – Distinctive and Diverse

Swabia has no real geographic or cultural-historical unity. Its present-day geographical confines are far more the result of historical developments and political and administrative decisions that were made without taking its geographical or linguistic borders into account. On the map, it resembles a narrow rectangle. The longest section, from south to north, is roughly 200 kilometres, and it is approximately 50 kilometres from west to east. With a surface area of around 10,000 square metres Swabia is the third-largest administrative division of Bavaria, and in population terms (roughly 1.78 million) the second-largest after Upper Bavaria. Apart from four towns administered as districts in their own right – (Augsburg, Kaufbeuren, Kempten and Memmingen), there are 334 parishes in 10 districts and 3 planning regions. Swabia has a share of the three great structural elements of Southern Germany: homoclinal ridges and escarpments in the north, alpine foothills in the middle, and the Alps themselves in the south. Within these basic geological and tectonic structures, various different forms of landscape can be clearly detected. To a large extent, the cultural development of the region has been strongly influenced by the diversity of its landscape.

The Ries

The Ries is an almost circular basin between 20 and 25 millimetres across, located in the Swabian and Franconian Jura ranges. The rivers Eger and Wörnitz and their numerous tributaries divide up the interior of the Ries into broad plains and flat depressions, dominated by 50 to 80-metre high elevations and hills around their edges. The vegetation is highly varied and species-rich, with grass and woodland, while the plains are covered with tilled fields and the depressions contain meadows.

This peaceful landscape gives no hint of the terrific disaster that created it – a massive meteorite impact. Granite and gneiss – normally found as crystalline rock 600 metres below ground – protrude above the surface at numerous locations. The rock accessible from above ground is often badly damaged, and the original seams have been shattered at several locations. At the edge of the Ries, pre-Tertiary sediment lies above younger rocks mixed with large chunks that have often been fused together into a specific lithified stone known as breccia. One unique Ries rock is the socalled suevite, or »Swabian stone«, its grey and porous mass interspersed with molten glass-like fragments; the rock closely resembles tuff, one of the reasons why the Ries was long considered to be of volcanic origin.

The various theories about the basin having been formed from something within the earth itself changed abruptly when suevite was found to contain minerals that can only be created by the intense heat of a meteorite collision. Further investigation gradual-

ly proved that the collision took place around 14.6 million years ago. An asteroid measuring roughly 1 kilometre across, and travelling at a speed of around 70,000 kilometres an hour, penetrated the atmosphere in less than 2 seconds and plunged up to 1 kilometre beneath the earth's rocky surface. The enormous energy released by this collision – the equivalent of roughly 250,000 atomic bombs of the type used at Hiroshima – pulverised not only the meteorite but also the surrounding rock, then melted it and vaporised it. Huge amounts of rock were hurled out of the crater, some of them landing up to 40 kilometres away. The hollow crater filled with water, and then a shallow lake formed which was gradually filled with limestone, sand and clay.

When large areas of Southern Germany were raised at the end of the Tertiary Period, the rivers cut through the surface, washing away the soft sediment and revealing the former crater shape once more. Individual hills made of hard Ries limestone appeared.

Eventually, the end of the last Ice Age gave the Ries loess deposits which, combined with a relatively dry, summery climate, have benefited agriculture in the region for millennia. Numerous relics from prehistory have proven the long duration and great continuity of settlement in the area. Thanks to its central location, the imperial city of Nördlingen developed into the economic and cultural centre of the Ries. Oettingen and Wallerstein played an important role as residences of the Counts of Oettingen, while Harburg and Wemding attained local importance.

The Swabian-Franconian Jura

Barren, poor soil and a scarcity of water are the main features of the Jura, a mountain range consisting of whitish-grey limestone and dolomite that crosses the whole of South Germany. It has all the features of a karst landscape, such as caverns and dry valleys, all of them produced by the softness and porosity of the local limestone. The sandy-clay soil and the various areas of rock flung outwards by the meteorite impact have benefited agriculture considerably, however, and resulted in regular settlement of the region throughout the ages.

The section of the Ries nearest the River Danube is noticeably water-rich: here, the rivers Egau, Kessel and Ussel have cut valleys through the high plain. The meadows here are luxuriant, and the numerous ploughed fields reveal the large amount of clay in the soil. Areas with less agricultural potential are used as grazing land for sheep. Large areas of predominantly sandy soil dating from the Tertiary Period have retained extensive forests. The valley of the River Wörnitz, traditionally considered to be the border between the Swabian and Franconian Jura, cuts 100 metres deep into the Jura range and has some impressive rock formations. Small villages and hamlets are a common sight here, while houses once characteristic of the Jura region have now largely disappeared.

The Danube Valley

The Jura descends as a sloping incline downwards to the Danube Valley. The Swabian section of this

Photos: Olav
König, Krumbach

1. Grey heron beside a dead arm of the Danube
2. Mindel and 3. The western Günz
4. Wild boar in the district of Dillingen
5. The Danube with remains of river forest between Altisheim/Lechsend
6. The carnation variety Dianthus superior, Hundsmoor
7. New Forest Burnet butterfly
8. Dry heathland, juniper bushes on Jurassic limestone in the Swabian Jura
9. Leucojum vernum, or Spring Snowflake
10. A carnation variety in the Benninger Ried
11. Common frog, rana temporaria
12. River woodland scene in the Donaumoos
13. Erratic block in the Kempter Forest – a relic of the Iller Glacier
14. Western Günz near Hawangen
15. Common river mussel (Unio crassus)

roughly 100-kilometre-long valley is distinctive for its breadth and space, and is located between the mouth of the Iller near Neu-Ulm and the mouth of the Lech near Marxheim. The width of the valley, and the metres-thick gravel beds below are the result of powerful streams of meltwater, brought in by the numerous southern tributaries during the Ice Ages. The bends in the old tributaries are evidence of powerful erosion, as is the sand and gravel piled up across the entire width of the valley. This river once used to be wild, but has now been tamed by regulation and construction: the water has been forced inside a canal-like channel and is now being used to generate power at a series of barrages.

These technical changes have also altered the forest that used to line the riverbanks. The four vertical vegetation levels – from the soil level to the herb and then the tree level – were once a perfect environment for all kinds of plants and animals, but their original form has only been retained in a few surviving sections. These are now valuable ecological islands, and are the breeding-grounds for innumerable species of bird.

Beyond the riverside forests there were once extensive areas of flat moorland, known in Swabia as Riede. They formed wherever a high level of groundwater, or standing water, led to the formation of peat. Removal of the peat over the past hundred years, combined with cultivation and draining, has now largely transformed these areas into luxuriant fields and meadows. The highly varied Ried-style vegetation, with its wild flowers and orchids, can still be found on the few stretches of original land that still remain.

Since medieval times, clay-covered gravel beds have developed into favourable locations for farms and small settlements. The settlements known as Schwaigen formerly existed on the islands in the Danube between Höchstädt and Donauwörth, but they lost their original role as cattle centres for cheese production and became normal farms when the grazing land was ploughed up for agriculture. A different landscape that also belongs to the Danube Valley is separated from the river level itself by a 5 to 10-metre-high terrace: the high terrace, which runs on the south side from Fahlheim to

7

10

13

15

11

14

8

9

12

Photo right:
Arbeitsgemeinschaft
Schwäbisches
Donaumoos

Günzburg, and on the north side from Langenau to Donauwörth. The layers of loess above the Ice Age gravel have turned them into a fertile landscape, with attractive villages and intensive agriculture. In between, separated by distances of 5 to 10 kilometres, lie several historic towns: Ulm/Neu-Ulm, Leipheim, Günzburg, Gundelfingen, Lauingen, Dillingen, Höchstädt and Donauwörth. The large number of towns here points to the great political importance of this region in medieval times.

The Tertiary Hills East of the Lower Lech

To the east of the River Lech, in the district of Aichach-Friedberg, Swabia also shares part of the Tertiary hills. This region was neither reached by the ice sheets nor covered by Ice-Age gravel. The Aindling terrace, in the lower part of the Lech, is the only area with any deposits dating from that era. The remainder was built up exclusively by the marl, sand and gravel from the Tertiary Period. Numerous rivers and streams have shaped the subsoil into undulating hill country with broad ranges, flat summits and wide valleys.

Loess soil provides good preconditions for agriculture in several places. The forests are largely limited to the hillsides. Wherever the subsoil consists of rough quartz sands, extensive forests of spruce and pine have developed. Different forms of farming, all of them dependent on geographical relief and soil suitability, have contributed much to the distinctive patchwork-like appearance of this landscape, which is very different from the clearly laid-out, almost schematic arrangements on the Iller-Lech plate. The Paar – the main river in the region – has cut a broad valley, along which main railway lines and roads now run. Villages, hamlets and lone farms are relatively evenly distributed across the region. Friedberg and Aichach are the historic centres of population here, as well as the main industrial towns.

Central Swabia – Terraced Landscape Between the Iller and Lech Rivers

In contrast to the smooth surface formations of the Danube Valley, the landscape further south gains gradually in energy and dynamism. The broad and deep valleys of the Lech, Wertach, Mindel, Günz and Iller, and the narrower Schmutter, Zusam, Kammel or Glött are separated from each other by long ranges of hills and undulating high plains. River valleys and ridge formations run strictly south-north and parallel to each other, gradually descending from the Alps to the Danube.

This relief was created by water that flowed during the Ice Ages. The rhythm of numerous cold and warm climatic periods caused alternation between a build-up of gravel and erosion of the subsoil. The reasons for the numerous changes in the climate over the past 2.5 million years have still not been fully explained. Continental drift, fluctuations in the Earth's orbit around the sun, and possibly even changes in the composition of the atmosphere could all have played a role. During the cold spells the annual temperatures sank by roughly 10 degrees, and the periods of sunshine were briefer. A large amount of winter precipitation remained on the ground as snow, before turning into ice, covering the Alps as glaciers and penetrating the area of the alpine foothills.

The erosive power of the scraping and gouging ice was most effective in the alpine valleys and also along the edge of the Alps. The valleys in the areas bordering directly to the north were created by thawing ice-rivers, and then covered with layers of gravel. The rivers repeatedly cut their way through the masses of detritus, leaving boulders and gravel behind on the valley floors as their power gradually weakened.

The gravel in the region between the Lech and the Iller lies at different heights and can be dated to at least six different Ice Ages; the strata are named after the alpine rivers Biber, Danube, Günz, Mindel, Riss and Würm. The sediment from the oldest Ice Age can be found on the surface of highest ranges of hills and summits, while the youngest gravel types from the following cold periods are situated further down. During the penultimate ice age – the Riss age – the glaciers moved very far north. An edge made up of ancient moraines reveal the maximum extent of the ice, which in the Lech and Wertach valley reached as far as a line between Bad Wörishofen and Kaufering, and also penetrated the region around Mering in the form of the Ammersee Glacier.

The last and most recent layers were deposited in the valleys of today's rivers during the Würm age. They can be detected along the Lech, Wertach and Iller as broad areas of gravel and boulders (Lech Plain, Wertach Plain), and also cover the valley floors of the Günz, Mindel, Roth and Iller. The Augsburg »Westliche Wälder« nature reserve, between the Danube, Wertach and Mindel rivers, is a good example of this Central Swabian terraced landscape.

Above: Undulating landscape in Central Swabia near Hinterschellenbach in the Westliche Wälder nature reserve near Augsburg.
Right: A view of the Cistercian convent and folk museum of Oberschönenfeld, nestling in the natural landscape of the Schwarzach valley, and surrounded by fields, meadows and forests. The Schmutter valley with Gessertshausen and Diedorf can be seen in the background.
Facing page: A view across the Alpsee near Immenstadt. The lake, which fills a valley gouged out by glaciers during the Riss period, lies among the forests and grassy slopes of the Allgäuer Vorberge.

The broad, furrowed valleys have been settlement and transport routes since time immemorial. The terraces higher up, covered with loess and out of reach of flood water, were the most preferred, as were the flat valley slopes; forests tended to predominate on the higher plains. Characteristic forms of settlement include the Haufendorf type of village, with unstructured distribution of houses and roads, and also the Wegedorf or wayside village

with its evenly patterned houses along both sides of a straight or slightly curving transport route.

Good transport connections have always played an important role in trade, and continue to determine the location of centres of industry even today. The triangle at the mouths of the Lech and Wertach rivers on the edge of the Lech Plain was a perfect location in this respect: Augsburg was first a Roman provincial capital, then a medieval town of craftsmen and traders, and is now an important industrial city. During the 20th century, numerous centres of settlement and industry sprang up around it including Gersthofen, Neusäss, Bobingen and Königsbrunn. Similarly well-situated from the traffic point of view is the Ulm/Neu-Ulm region, where the Iller and the Blau reach the Danube, and the settlement continues along the Iller valley in the towns of Senden, Vöhringen and Illertissen. The long, high ridges and numerous rivers presented great obstacles to east-west traffic. The old Roman route from Salzburg to Augsburg and Strasbourg was followed during the Middle Ages by the important salt road via Augsburg and Günzburg. Later, railways and motorways both followed roughly the same route. In the transition region from gravel terraces to the moraine landscape of the alpine foothills, nature also provided the basis for a suitable east-west connection. The towns of Landsberg, Mindelheim and Memmingen all sprang up at regular intervals along the important trading and salt routes. Indeed, Memmingen was very fortunately situated at the junction of two important long-distance routes, and this did much to promote it to the status of free imperial city.

The Alpine Foothills and Moraine Landscape

The landscape of Southern Swabia is complex. Long ranges of hills, broad summits and flat basins alternate with each other in a confined area, and the courses of rivers or the width of valleys can change within a very short distance. The relief is the result of the scraping and gouging action of glacial ice and meltwater erosion. From the Lech valley came the Lech Glacier, which left the mountains near Füssen and Pfronten and extended up to 40 kilometres across the alpine foothills of the Eastern Allgäu. From the Iller valley came the Iller Glacier, which only managed to expand around 20 kilometres north of Immenstadt because of limitation by glacial folds. From the alpine valley of the Rhine came the enormous Rhine Glacier, which covered the Lake Constance basin and beyond with mighty ice-rivers and also penetrated the north and west, reaching widths of over 100 kilometres in places. Together with the narrower Ammersee Glacier and Wertach Glacier, it formed a thick ice sheet across the entire alpine foothill region.

During the period of maximum elevation in the Riss and Würm ages, the ice sheet closest to the mountains reached to heights of between 1200 and 1500 metres. Towards the north, the ice masses gradually thinned out, and piled up the boulders and detritus they carried with them into massive moraines. A long range of hills extending across the whole of Swabia from Kaufbeuren to Obergünzberg and Altusried resembles a garland, and marks the farthest extent of the glacier during the Würm age. Within the moraine walls, the large boulders and powdered rock carried along by the glacier form the so-called ground moraine. The main basins of the glaciers often preserved large lakes (e. g. the Weissensee, Hopfensee, Bannwaldsee and Niedersonthofener See), although former lakes near Wertach, Marktoberdorf and Unterthingau have long since drained away. Other relics of the Ice Age include such small basins as the Elbsee, the Seeger lakes and the numerous ponds and moors. In the basin of Lake Constance, gouged out deeply by the mighty Rhine Glacier, one of the largest lakes of this region remained. The ridges and hills of the Allgäu fold tower above the 700 to 800-metre-high moraine landscape. These higher sections belong geologically and tectonically to the Alps themselves, but morphologically they also form a considerable part of the alpine foothill region. To the west of the Iller they can be found in numerous closely-packed chains (Hauchenberg-Stoffelberg, or the Halmaser range), and form the gradual transition to the mountains. To the east of the Iller, together with the Wertach Ridge and the Senkele-Zwieselberg chain, they feature several striking-looking elevations.

Below: View from the Oberjoch across the sea of fog in the Ostrach and Iller valleys. The Flysch Mountains in the Hörner group can be seen to the left, and the high peaks of the Nagelfluh range dominate the background. The picture provides an impression of the situation during the Ice Age 20,000 years ago, when glaciers filled the valleys just as the fog does now. Facing page: View from the Faulensee near Füssen of the rough, jagged peaks of the Säuling and Vilser Alps.

Settlement and deforestation have reduced the forest in the region, which now covers the moraines, steep valley slopes and mountainsides. Forest has also been preserved beside the rivers and streams. The open countryside is being intensively tilled, or used for mowing. When people realized during the mid-19th century that the soil and climate conditions were best suited to grazing land, the ploughed areas south of the terminal moraines disappeared almost completely. The settlement pattern is marked by hamlets and individual farmsteads that date back to the forest clearance of the 16th to 18th centuries. Rural markets and villages form the local centres. The former imperial cities of Kempten and Kaufbeuren have now developed into administrative and industrial centres with excellent transport connections. The island town of Lindau on Lake Constance occupies a special position as far as location and function are concerned.

The Allgäu Alps

The Allgäu Alps rise ever higher in an impressive series of ranges. Their geological structure is complex, but bears the distinctive features of a fold with various components and several consecutive layers. The stone sediment left behind by the Triassic Period is dominated by greyish-brown dolomite, while the Jurassic has produced a special form of dark-brown marl. Much sand and slate has been left behind by the Cretaceous, while the Tertiary has given us sandstone and clay and has contributed much to producing the outer regions of today's Alps. All this sediment, collected in different sea basins under varying conditions during the course of more than 200 million years, was brought to the surface by large-scale movements of the earth's crust, predominantly during the Tertiary Period – after which it was subjected to weathering and erosion.

As far as natural areas are concerned, two can be discerned that have been separated by the broad valley of the river Iller. The so-called limestone foothills (10–15 kilometres wide) are the mountains to the west of the river that reach their highest elevation at the Hochgrat, Rindalphorn and Stuiben, and also the gently formed mountains of the Hörner group in the south. To the east of the Iller there are several east-west mountain ridges between Wertach, Nesselwang, Pfronten, Füssen and Trauchgau. Their summits are gently rounded and usually forested. Flat areas and the gentler slopes have been deforested for the purposes of dairy farming, and the settlements are usually beneath the 800-metre line. The predominantly cool, damp and rainy climate limits agricultural use; it led to a specialization in cattle farming as long ago as medieval times.

The historic towns of Immenstadt and Füssen grew up at favourable transport locations, and Sonthofen, situated in the broad valley of the Iller, developed into a garrison town and administrative centre. The influence of tourism has turned numerous valley towns such as Fischen, Hindelang, Oberstaufen, Nesselwang, Pfronten and Schwangau into attractive spas and holiday centres. The entire Upper Allgäu is also famous for all the snow it gets, and the winter season here is just as popular as the summer one.

Towards the south lies the zone of the high limestone Alps, rising from gentle slopes to the strikingly-shaped high mountain ridges and peaks over 2000 metres above sea-level. The various different Ice Ages have left numerous fascinating shapes behind: rough rock-faces, pointed peaks, and scree-covered slopes. Further down, deciduous trees are still the formative landscape feature, but the pine forests begin a little higher up. The natural tree-line has often been altered by deforestation. Meadows and high pastures are used for intensive alpine dairy farming. Sharp differences in relief and a high amount of precipitation in the summer have limited the settlement potential here to only a few areas (the Oberstdorf basin, the Walser valley, the Füssener Bucht and the Pfrontener Becken). The highest permanently populated settlement here is the hamlet of Gerstruben, 1100 metres above sea level.

Hans Frei

Prehistoric Swabia in Pictures

The Swabian landscape contains a great wealth of prehistoric remains. These are important sources of information for archaeologists, documenting a period that left us nothing in writing. The almost 8000 archaeological sites in Swabia span more than 10000 years of settlement and cultural history, and the objects recovered are on display in numerous civic and folk museums.

Stone implements and tools made from bone provide proof of settlement since the Old Stone Age. Ceramic mugs, jugs and bowls are important clues to settlement and cultural patterns during recent prehistory, when lasting settlements were founded, plants cultivated and cattle bred. The different periods are marked clearly by the varying patterns and shapes of vessel. The Bronze and Iron Age cultures used metals to make tools, weapons and jewellery. A number of vessels discovered near Unterglauheim in the district of Dillingen included two bronze cauldrons and two golden bowls inside a large bronze container, all of them very skilfully crafted. Substantial finds from burial mounds provide an insight into life during the Hallstatt Period. Numerous relics of the Celts, a people that had a strong influence on European culture, survive from the final centuries BC. The Romans ruled the area between the Ries and Lake Constance for almost 400 years, and this is represented by a large number of monuments and archaeological finds. Numerous centres of settlement can trace their origins back to Roman times: not only the provincial capital of Augusta Vindelicum, described by the Roman author Tacitus as »a magnificent city«, but also Füssen, Günzburg, Kempten, Nördlingen, Schwabmünchen and several others. Augsburg was a religious, administrative, military, commercial and craft centre. The remains of temples, statues and funerary slabs testify to the central role played by Augsburg during Roman times, and population of the surrounding countryside is documented by street villages, farms and cemeteries. All the long Roman roads were marked with milestones. After the Romans came the Alemannians, and it was they who founded most of the settlements as we know them today.

Hans Frei

Above right: Ceramic bowl, patterned with punctures and grooves, from the Hexenbergle burial mound between Bobingen and Wehringen, 8th century BC, Roman Museum, Augsburg.
Above: Hand-axe from Großsorheim, roughly 9 centimetres long, and used by Neanderthals in the Ries around 80,000 years ago.
Right: Bronze vessel, two bronze bowls and two decorated gold cups, 9th century BC, found at Unterglauheim in the district of Dillingen, and now on display in the Roman Museum in Augsburg.

Above left: Gilded bronze statuette of the Genius Populi Romani (height 45 cm), protector of the Roman state. It was probably part of a statue of the Emperor Claudius. First century AD, Roman Museum, Augsburg.
Above right: Life-sized horse's head from an equestrian statue, bronze, gilded, first half of the 2nd century AD, Roman Museum, Augsburg.
Left: Tomb slab of a wine merchant, showing a barrel being transported by ox-cart, ca. 200 AD, Jurassic limestone, Roman Museum, Augsburg.
Above: Fresco from a Roman house near Schwangau in the Ostallgäu district, second half of the 2nd century AD.

The Ries is surrounded by an arc-shaped range of hills, broken up by valleys that blend into each other. The arc is probably not entirely circular, but the landscape is of a rare unity and topographical harmony.

Albert Schlagbauer (1913–2001)

The Ries

Nördlingen is considered a model medieval town. Located at the junction of several important trading routes, the town developed into one of South Germany's most important business centres of the Late Middle Ages.

The view from the »Daniel« – the tower of St. George's Church – takes in the market square, town hall and the totally intact city wall, with its gates and towers.

Seldom has a landscape been praised as much as the Ries, that bowl-shaped depression between the Franconian and Swabian Jura. When the humanist Veit Ammerbacher from Wemding gave a speech about his fatherland at Wittenberg University in 1540, it turned into a hymn of praise for the Ries: »Before my eyes I can see my father's house, where I learned about the beginnings of religion and virtue, and about the surrounding area with all its springs, meadows, forests, mountains and orchards, which are particularly beautiful there. The town lies on the northern border of Rhaetia – the region still bears that name (Ries) – and no other stretch of land has such fertile soil or so many inhabitants.«

A little later, during the mid-16th century, Sebastian Münster praised the economic benefits of this landscape in his Cosmographia, mentioning all the cattle in the luxuriant meadows, the numerous different kinds of fruit, and the magnificent horses, geese, pigs and other animals in the region. Georg Monninger, the town clerk of Nördlingen, described the area in 1893: »One of the strangest regions of Swabia is the Ries. Enclosed by magnificent hills, connecting the Swabian and Franconian Jura ranges, it contains a large number of attractive and often historically interesting towns, and its plain is covered with monasteries, castles and villages. It is one of the most blessed regions of the fatherland.«

So Georg Monninger thought of this landscape as strange – and he was certainly right there, especially since he meant strange in the sense of intriguing rather than curious. Because the Ries is definitely an intriguing region.

First of all there is the unusual topography of the area, which posed a riddle to scientists and researchers for centuries. Was the almost circular, bowl-like landscape the result of a massive volcanic eruption, or was it created by a mighty glacier? This question preoccupied scientists throughout the 19th and 20th centuries, and was finally answered in 1960 by the American researchers Eugene Shoemaker and Edward Chao. While the two scientists were examining the stones in the Ries in preparation for the first moon landing, they discovered two minerals that are

There were 85 leather tanneries in Nördlingen's »Gerbergasse« streets during the Middle Ages. The last of the town's tanners worked at Gerbergasse 39 until 1961.

only produced under extreme pressure conditions – during a meteorite impact, for instance. The significance of the find was soon clear. Further discoveries corroborated the theory, and soon it was absolutely certain that the Ries was created by a meteorite that had crashed into the Earth 14.7 million years ago.

A cosmic collision of such proportions is hard to imagine. A meteorite approximately 1,000 metres wide penetrated the Earth's atmosphere at a speed of roughly 20 kilometres per second and plunged up to 1,000 metres beneath the Jurassic stone and crystalline rock. The meteorite and the surrounding rock were then crushed together into less than half of their original volume. Almost instantly, the so-called primary crater was formed – roughly 12 kilometres in diameter. The enormous pressure continued through the surrounding rock at above the speed of sound, but lost energy very quickly. The meteorite and the rock it hit both vaporised, but around 150 cubic metres of rock were flung out of the crater, and blocks of stone weighing several tons were hurled upward and outward, some of them landing up to 60 kilometres

Above: The Rotgerberhaus, built in around 1422, is one of the most impressive houses of its type. The drying floors of the former tannery are a typical feature.
Below: Half-timbered houses and baroque buildings are a distinctive feature of the old part of Oettingen. The Oettingen-Spielberg residence with its baroque outer façade and Italian Renaissance interior decoration is well worth a visit.

There are several architectural gems in the shadow of the town walls – such as this small house dating from the years following the Thirty Years' War.

Today Nördlingen has long outgrown its medieval walls. It was only several centuries after the losses of the Thirty Years' War that it managed to regain its original population figures.
In 1600 the town had 8,790 inhabitants, while in 1652 there were just 4,350. The figure from 1600 was only re-attained in 1939.

away. Depressions around the impact zone were the result, causing the crater diameter to widen to around 25 kilometres.

All plant and animal life for thousands of square kilometres around was obliterated. The huge crater filled up with water, however, from rain, groundwater and rivers. This produced a crater lake which lasted around two million years, but was gradually filled with sediment. It was only at the end of the Tertiary Period, when the Jura and parts of South Germany were lifted by tectonic movements that the numerous rivers and streams washed the sediment away and exposed the bowl shape once more. The Ries limestone withstood this erosion more strongly than the surrounding rock and was thus partially exposed in the form of hills. Loess and sand covered the base of the bowl during the Ice Ages, producing the natural basis for the Ries' reputation as »the granary of Bavaria«. During this era, around 80,000 years ago, man set foot in the Ries region for the first time. It was at this stage that the Ries underwent a transition from a natural landscape to a cultural landscape.

Today experts agree that the Ries is a prehistoric treasure trove, especially since it was continuously inhabited – something very unusual. The hand-axe discovered at Mündling on the edge of the region is over 130,000 years old, and the axe found at Grosssorheim is between 70,000 and 80,000 years old; both these items prove that the Ries and its environs were populated by hunters and gatherers. The skulls buried in the large and small Öfnet caves, and in the so-called »Witch's Kitchen« near Lierheim with funeral gifts from the Mediterranean region, make it clear how large a cultural area the Ries included. Another famous find was the limestone slab with scratched drawings from the Höhlenstein, along with numerous other items that can today be admired in the museums of Nördlingen, Bopfingen and Wemding.

In 90 BC, under the Emperor Domitian, the Ries and its northern region were incorporated into the Roman province of Rhaetia, from which the Ries originally derived its name. Continuous attacks by Alemannian tribes from 213 AD onwards forced the Romans to abandon their Rhaetian fortifications in around 260 AD and shift their sphere of influence to behind the River Danube. The Ries thus became a settlement area for the Alemannians, who discovered ideal conditions there: cultivated land and also a Roman infrastructure consisting of roads and farms. Large sections of the Roman road network were directly incorporated into the medieval routes, and still appear in significant sections of modern road maps too. Alongside the well-researched camps of Losodica (Munningen) and Opie (Oberdorf), Roman relics include around 100 estates. The foundation walls of the Roman estate beneath the Ofnet Caves in the Maienbach Valley have now been exposed, and provide an insight into the variety and size of the buildings at that time.

After the victory of the Frankish king Clovis I over the Alemannians in the year 496, a new, Frankish phase of settlement began in the Ries. It was accompanied by far-reaching cultural, political and social changes. Both the Alemannian and Frankish settlement had an impact on the fundamental structure of the Ries.

Today it is known that the basic pattern of settlement in the Ries was determined during this phase of Alemannian-Frankish occupation. The villages at that time were generally small settlements made up of several farmsteads. Some noble families settled in these villages, and the remains of their houses can sometimes be seen, frequently accompanied by the ruins of later buildings on the same site.

These noble families, from local nobles all the way to important

Above: An imperial synod called together by King Conrad I met in Hohenaltheim in the year 916. Only ruins remain of the church of St. John the Baptist at that time – today's structure dates from the period around 1360. It was extended in the mid-18th century.
Right: The birthplace of the doctor and botanist Leonhard Fuchs (1501–1566) stands in the market square of Wemding. A famous flower, the fuchsia, was named after him.

Above: The church of Maria Brünnlein is one of the most popular pilgrimage destinations in Bavaria. Its origins date back to the miraculous powers of a statue of the Virgin Mary that a cobbler from Wemding brought back to the town from a pilgrimage to Rome in 1684. The foundation stone was laid in 1748, and the church was completed in 1752. Left: In the courtyard of the Residenz castle in Oettingen, visitors will find the section of the former castle known as the Alte Münz. Below: Niederhaus Castle once belonged to the von Hürnheims before it was transferred to the von Oettingen family at the end of the 17th century. In 1709 the Teutonic Order acquired the castle after it had been partially destroyed during the Thirty Years' War.

landowners, were the people who determined – together with the churches and monasteries and also the local population – how the settlement pattern would continue to develop. Despite all social changes, the pattern remained largely the same. It was only the socio-economic transformations during the 20th century that brought sometimes worrying alterations to the pattern of settlement, which are continuing to have an impact on the landscape.

The Ries can certainly be termed a landscape full of castles and fortresses. Or to put it another way: where would the Ries be today without its numerous ruined castles, hunting lodges and summer residences? In the mid-12th century the noble families of von Oettingen, von Hürnheim, von Lierheim and von Hohenburg – the most powerful noble families during the High Middle Ages – entered history for the first time. They have all disappeared long since, apart from the von Oettingen family – but impressive ruins of their former castles and residences still remain.

The real highlight of the Ries is without doubt the massive Harburg fortress, high above the valley of the Wörnitz and the small town of the same name. It is, after all, one of the largest and best-preserved castles in all of Germany. This Hohenstaufen fortress, first mentioned in documents in 1150, became the property of the von Oettingen family in 1299 as the result of a pledge. Thousands of visitors come here every year when they catch sight of the imposing-looking castle with its many towers, high above the Romantic Road. The famous German artist Carl Spitzweg was also delighted by the Harburg and its idyllic location, and did several sketches of it in 1858 during a journey through the region.

Baldern Castle lies in the part of the Ries that belongs to the state of Baden-Württemberg. It is not only striking for its exposed location on a cone-shaped hill with a fantastic panoramic view, but also for its comprehensive weapons collection. Like the Harburg and Wallerstein Castle, Baldern Castle is also the property of the von Oettingen-Wallerstein family, who were ennobled in 1774.

Any tour of the von Oettingen family's residences and castles is best rounded off by a visit to the town of Oettingen itself, formerly the location of their family seat. The castle was built during the High Middle Ages, and by the 15th and 16th centuries it had become an impressive fortress complex before its demolition in the 19th century. The Protestant line of Oettingen-Oettingen princes resided here until they died out in 1731. At the other end of the town, however, at the end of Schlossstrasse (Castle Street), the castle of the noble family of Oettingen-Spielberg still stands. It received its present-day appearance between 1678 and 1687. The architecture of the market square and main street – with half-timbered houses on one side and baroque houses on the other – was based on this castle and the medieval town hall.

One town, with two castles! This special feature of Oettingen dates back to the division of an inheritance among the town's counts at the beginning of the 15th century. It made it necessary to establish two castles, two administrations, two churches, and so forth. And when one of the two lines decided to adopt the Protestant faith during the Reformation, the town also became religiously divided.

Not only the fortresses and castles but also the towns are distinctive features of the Ries. Not every town is alike, however: the residence town of Oettingen, the fortress town of Harburg and the Bavarian provincial towns of Bopfingen and Nördlingen all have to be carefully differentiated: their appearance and architecture alone contrast greatly. The former imperial city of Nördlingen is an exemplary medieval town in which every feature of a community during the Middle Ages has been preserved to the present day. The church and town hall are at the centre, and are surrounded by fully preserved fortifications made up of moats, ditches, gates and towers; there is a municipal monastery, a hospital, craftsmen's houses and workshops, a leather-tanning quarter, granaries and storehouses, townhouses belonging to wealthy merchants, inns and taverns. Visitors can experience all these features of a medieval town »live«, as it were, even though the outlying

Left: The buildings of Wallerstein Castle, together with the grounds, riding school and other outbuildings, provide an impressive insight into the country life of the nobility during the 18th and 19th centuries.

areas of Nördlingen have now turned it into an important industrial site. History fans will find a treasure-trove of information in the museums located within the old town walls: around 90,000 people visit these museums each year to gain a deeper insight into various different aspects of the town's history.

Churches and monasteries are further highlights of the cultural mosaic that makes up the Ries. It is no exaggeration to say that art lovers can see a truly enormous amount of church and monastery treasures in this region. Benedictines settled here just as much as Carthusians, Cistercians, Franciscans and Carmelites. The oldest monastery in the Ries is Mönchsdeggingen, which according to monastery tradition dates back to a foundation by the Emperor Otto the Great. Documentation proves that the Emperor Heinrich II made over the village and monastery of Deggingen in 1007 and 1016 to the bishopric of Bamberg, which ran the monastery from then onwards. The noble family of Hürnheim-Hochhaus then governed it until 1347, when they sold their Hochhaus Castle together with stewardship of the monastery to the Counts of Oettingen. The former monastery church, with its ornate baroque decoration, is one of the finest in the Ries. It is just as popular a destination as the pilgrimage church of Maria Brünnlein near Wemding, which is visited by thousands of people every year. The church, now elevated to the status of a basilica minor, was attractively renovated in 1999.

The benefits of cross-regional promotion have recently been recognized in this part of Germany: to combine the cultural power of the two districts of Donauwörth and Nördlingen, the Donau-Ries tourist authority was

One of the finest churches in the Ries: the monastery church of Mönchsdeggingen with its magnificent baroque stucco work and ceiling frescoes.

founded in 1999. And with good reason, because this unique landscape with the Ries crater at its heart is more than worthy of increased recognition.

The Ries was once referred to as »Bavaria's granary«, but today agriculture is on the wane, and new resources are being tapped. There is a great deal to be discovered, and »marketed«. Not only in the sphere of art, culture and architecture, but also with regard to personalities famed far beyond the region. One of them is the Oettingen-born Hieronymus Wolf (1526–1581), the founder of Byzantine studies, or that great friend of Goethe Karl Ludwig von Knebel, who was born in Wallerstein Castle in 1744. Another person worthy of mention is William Berczy, also born in Wallerstein in 1744, who was one of the co-founders of Toronto.

The historian and legal expert Karl Heinrich Ritter von Lang, whose memoirs became very famous, was born in the parsonage of Balgheim in 1764; and Wilhelm Ludwig Wekhrlin (1739–1792), one of the most brilliant satirists of the 18th century, was also born in the Ries. The latter had to be placed in protective custody by the Prince of Wallerstein after he had fallen into such disfavour with the town of Nördlingen that he feared for his life. This is just a small selection of »local Ries celebrities« – the list can definitely be extended much further.

Any description of a landscape as many-faceted as the Ries must necessarily remain fragmentary. It is impossible to provide more than a fleeting impression here. Melchior Meyr (1810–1871) once attempted to sum up the special quality possessed by the people of the Ries: »A description of a tribe, indeed only a fraction of a tribe that forms a whole in itself, is a task that can never be regarded as solved ...« And it is for precisely that reason that people should travel to the Ries themselves, and form their own opinion of its inhabitants!

Wilfried Sponsel

Right: The Harburg towers high above the Wörnitz River, on a rocky outcrop. It gained its present appearance after a series of structural phases dating from the 13th to the 18th century.
Left: The picturesque little town of Harburg has numerous idyllic corners. The Wörnitz Bridge, which gained its present-day appearance in 1729, connects the two sides of the town – which has long outgrown its old centre below the castle.

Those interested in gaining familiarity with Swabia's beauty and culture need not necessarily follow the beaten tourist track. To the east and west of the Romantic Road, the Northern Swabian towns from Ulm to Neuburg are definitely worth a visit. The fertile landscape between Ries and Donauried, the delightful unity of the historic towns, the large number of architecturally important monuments, the high standard of local as well as international cuisine in the many restaurants here, and above all the excellent Danube cycling route, which follows the great river from Donaueschingen to Ulm, Regensburg, Vienna and Budapest, have all made this region a major tourist success.

Indeed, cycling is probably one of the best ways of appreciating the delights here: the sleepy old towns, the rare birdlife of the Ried, and the huge skies above this thinly-populated part of Germany. It can easily be reached by car or train, of course, along the B16 or the Danube Valley route from Ulm to Regensburg respectively. This region has excelled itself by cherishing cultural traditions on the one hand while remaining open to innovative progress on the other.

The comparatively mild temperatures probably also explain why the towns located along the River Danube here are so close to one another. For the Romans, the river was an important barrier against potential Germanic incursions, and even later, decisions were made in this part of Europe that had a decisive effect on the continent's history as a whole.

One example of living history is Leitheim Castle, situated to the east of Donauwörth. The Leitheimer Schlosskonzerte, organised since 1959, are a magnet for music fans from the cultural cities of Bavaria and Baden-Württemberg. In the late 17th century the building was constructed high above the Danube by Kaisheim's Cistercian monks as a summer residence, before being extended half a century later and turned into a magnificent example of the Bavarian Rococo style. Since 1835, Leitheim Castle has been owned by the Tucher family (directly descended from the famous Tuchers of Nuremberg), and has been open to the public for roughly 40 years. Its valuable exhibits include the cross worn by Mary Queen of Scots on the day she died.

The Danube Towns

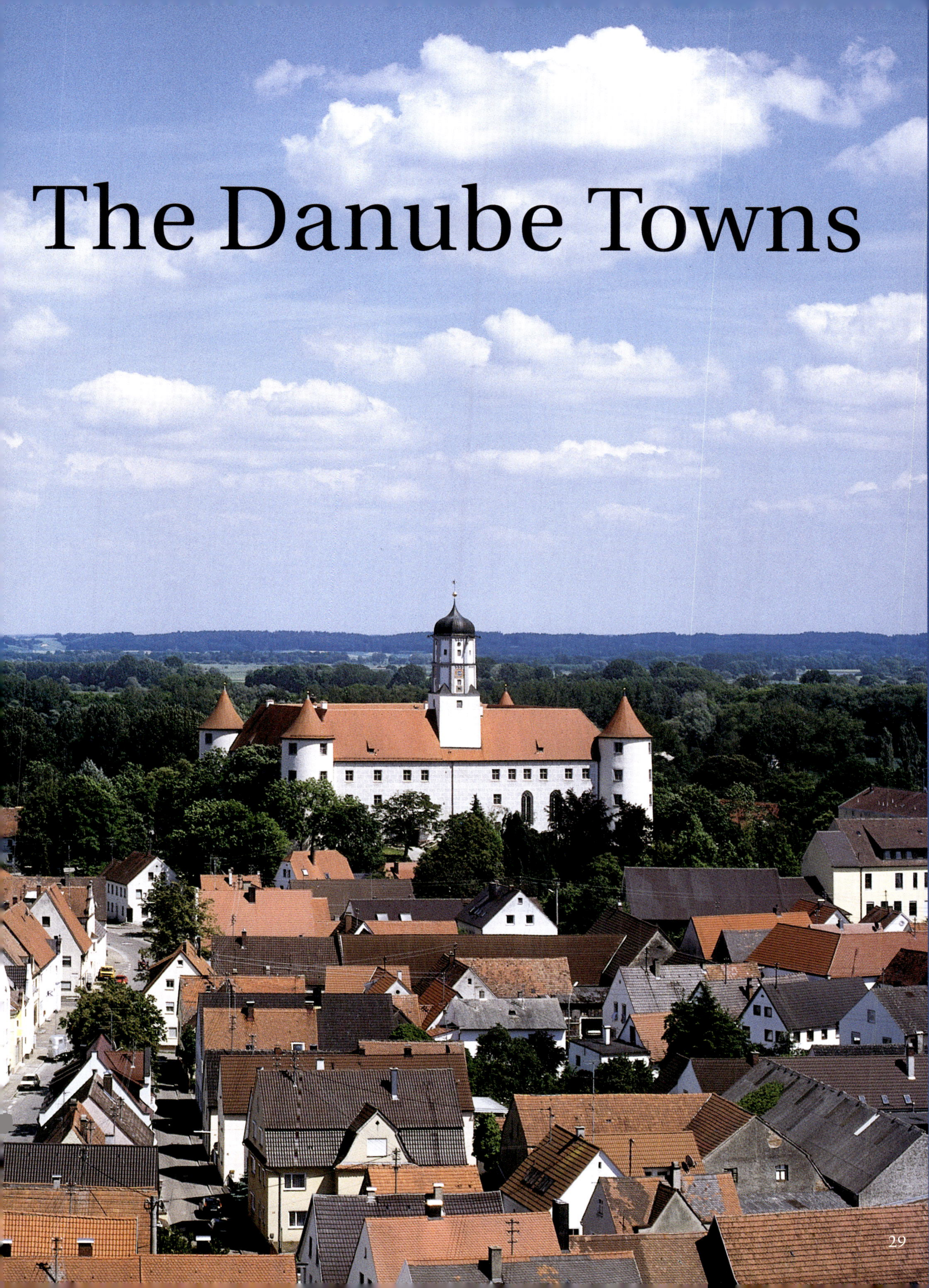

Pages 28/29: The Renaissance Castle of Höchstädt towers high above the town and the Danube Plain.
Pages 30/31 from left: Visitors to the Danube towns of Northern Swabia encounter historic architecture and idyllic scenery every step of the way. Leitheim Castle, formerly a summer residence of the Kaisheim Cistercian Order, is famed for its concerts.
The Färbertörl Tower in Donauwörth stands as a reminder of the town's former fortifications.
Although numerous innovative companies are based in Donauwörth, photographers can still find all kinds of picturesque motifs – such as here at the confluence of the Danube and the Wörnitz.

Travelling up the Danube we reach Donauwörth, the first of the Northern Swabian cities to line the northern bank of the river at brief intervals. Donauwörth, first mentioned in documents in 1030, has preserved or rebuilt much of its historical substance, despite suffering serious bomb damage in April 1945. It is famed for its Reichsstrasse, which was already part of the transport network of the Holy Roman Empire of German Nations; its Deutschordenshaus, one of the oldest meeting places of the German order of knights; the Stadtkommandantenhaus, rebuilt in 1950 after its destruction during World War II; the Tanzhaus (Dance House), a social centre of the former free imperial city; and the Gothic brick Church of Our Dear Lady with its three naves, its Gothic frescoes and the Pummerin, the largest church-bell in all of Swabia.

Donauwörth became especially important just before the Thirty Years' War, when a conflict between Protestants and Catholics in 1608 prompted the Emperor Rudolph to place the city under a ban, which the Bavarian duke Maximilian I was told to execute. At this point several estates of the Empire joined together under the leadership of the Electoral Palatinate to form the Protestant Union. One year later, the Catholic League was formed. The die was now cast, and it merely took the Defenestration of Prague in 1618 to spark off the conflict.

Donauwörth's location on the Romantic Road and its importance as a rail traffic centre have both clearly had a positive influence on its development as a regional town. Its economic ascendancy in the district of Donau-Ries is reflected in the high number of modern businesses that have settled

here, such as the famous Eurocopter GmbH. The factory is part of a German-French combine that is famous as the world's largest helicopter manufacturer.

Between Donauwörth and Höchstädt, federal highway 16 passes the town of Donaumünster, which has a local castle closely associated with the name Alexander von Bernus (1880–1965). As editor of the magazine Freistatt (1902–1905), the painter and alchemist was good friends with such famous authors as Ricarda Huch, Else Laske-Schüler, F. Wedekind, F. Blei, R. M. Rilke, P. Scheerbart, Stefan Zweig, Thomas Mann and Hermann Hesse. It was at the castle in Donaumünster that Bernus spent his final years. In 1995 the Alexander von Bernus Society was founded here with the aim of preserving the poet's extensive œuvre.

Höchstädt's mighty Renaissance castle towers high above the Danube plain. It was built in the late 16th century by Philipp Ludwig, the third duke of the young princedom of Palatinate-Neuburg. The four-winged structure encloses an almost square-shaped inner courtyard, and the three-storey building's outer corners are flanked by four round towers. The castle keep – all that remains of the earlier medieval structure – is a striking feature. This castle had its heyday between 1616 and 1632, when Anna of Jülich, Cleves and Berg, the widow of Philipp Ludwig, brought courtly splendour to the town. After various phases as an administration building, prison, police station and old people's home, the castle stood empty for almost 20 years from 1967 onwards. Today the ground floor houses the »Forum for Swabian History«, created by the district of Swabia for organising cultural events and special exhibitions.

The former residence and university town of Dillingen has successfully preserved its historic centre over the centuries.
From left: the Königstrasse with its Mitteltor Tower is still the main thoroughfare in Dillingen.
Chairs outside a café in front of Dillingen's town hall provide a southern atmosphere during the hot summers.
The former university building in Dillingen today houses the Bavarian Academy for Teacher Training.
The mighty towers of Dillingen castle, formerly the residence of the prince-bishops of Augsburg.

Various pieces of military equipment keep cropping up today in the fields to the east of the town, all of them reminders of the Battle of Höchstädt (1704). Winston Churchill visited the site on two occasions, and British elite soldiers are also regular visitors to the place where the Battle of Blenheim was fought. A monument just outside the town on the road to Blindheim commemorates those who died in the battle that was won decisively by Prince Eugen, and gave the Spanish War of Secession its decisive turn.

The town of Dillingen has developed into the social centre of the entire Dillingen district. It reached the height of its fortunes during the 16th, 17th and 18th centuries, when Jesuits turned its university into a famous centre of the Counter-Reformation. It was thanks to a decision by the prince-bishops of Augsburg that Dillingen became a university town: during the Reformation they shifted their residence to the reliably Catholic town and turned it into a »Swabian Rome«. The former glory of that epoch is still architecturally evident today. The mighty prince-episcopal castle and the Basilica of St. Peter are still the most striking landmarks in the old town centre. The Studienkirche, a church erected at the beginning of the 17th century, is a fine pilastered structure and one of the most important religious edifices in South Germany. This former university church rounds off the impressive main section of the former university, and is now a part of the Bavarian Teacher Training Academy. The courses at this institute are attended by teachers from all over Bavaria, many of whom are continuing important development work abroad in countries such as China, where similar teacher training centres are now being established.

Episcopal Dillingen and its Protestant neighbouring town of Lauingen in Palatinate-Neuburg used to be fierce enemies, but today nothing remains of their former rivalry apart from a few lines in cabaret texts. Indeed, the two towns almost have a joint centre. Lauingen's civic administration and also its townspeople are keen on cooperation and tolerance, and this was recently expressed in the town's architecture with the construction of a mosque for the town's Moslem community.

As the second town to be chosen as a residence by the dukes of Palatinate-Neuburg, Lauingen achieved great prosperity. The facades of the townhouses with their high gables, especially on the Herzog-Georg-Strasse, are clear expressions of bourgeois self-confidence, and the picturesque little corners of this town impress every visitor. The partly-restored Apollo Grannus Temple in Lauingen's western district of Faimingen is a reminder of the Romans' former presence here; they secured the Danube borders with a fort and Vicus Phoebiana. The title of the extensive Roman settlement here has only been known since 1981, when two milestones bearing the name were discovered beneath the parish church of Gundelfingen.

Gundelfingen, the fourth Danube town in the district of Dillingen, is a textbook example of successful urban restoration. The view through the arches of the Torturm Tower and down Professor-Bamann-Strasse can now be seen on innumerable photos. The centre, with its renovated townhouses, is clear proof that historical town centres can remain picturesque while continuing to fulfil all the requirements of modern shopping areas.

The Danube towns of Swabia feature all kinds of tourist attractions.
From left: Projecting gables resembling swallows' nests, such as these in the Untere Brunnental, are a characteristic feature of the former town wall in Lauingen.
A fine combination of renovated town centre and modern shops: the market square in Günzburg.
The beautifully restored Frauenkirche in Günzburg, one of the major masterpieces of Dominikus Zimmermann.
The interior of the Frauenkirche in Günzburg is famous as a »miracle of light«.

Here, too, local inhabitants and visitors alike encounter history with every step they take. The town's coat of arms is a reminder of the Hohenstaufen era when the community received its municipal charter, and the ruined fortifications testify to several attacks by enemies as well as to the special bravery of the Gundelfingers themselves. After their courageous resistance during the siege of the town by Margrave Albrecht Achilles in 1461/1462, Duke Ludwig the Rich of Bavaria granted the town a much-coveted privilege: its taxes were halved for a full 14 years.

Just outside Günzburg, Reisensburg Castle can be seen high on a hill above the Danube. This once-ruined castle dates back to Roman times, and long delighted the Romantics, but it was recently restored and turned into the International Institute for Scientific Cooperation. In 1989 the castle made the headlines when a summit between the German chancellor Helmut Kohl and the French president Francois Mitterrand was held there. In fact it was during that meeting that Mitterrand settled a French financial debt dating right back to the year 1805: Napoleon I had stayed in Günzburg, and had quite simply forgotten to pay a bill there – amounting to 423 guilders.

The town of Günzburg, located on the old postal route between Vienna and Paris, has been visited by VIPs throughout its history. The Habsburg princess Marie-Antoinette spent several days here during her bridal journey to Versailles, complete with 57 carriages and 370 horses. The regular flow of traffic

brought the town a great deal of money, and during the 18th century, 19 of the 43 houses around the market square were inns that were allowed to brew their own beer. From 1764 to 1767, today's town hall housed a mint that produced coins for Vorderösterreich, the Austrian provinces west of the Arlberg. The letters SF on the Maria Theresa thalers struck in Vienna are still reminders of Günzburg mintmasters Tobias Schöhl and Joseph Faby.

Today Günzburg and the town of Leipheim to the west of it form a centre. The local government reorganisation strengthened Günzburg's central location in Northwestern Swabia, and this function is also clear from its pulsing cultural life – conditions for which are ideal in the shape of the »Forum am Hofgarten«.

Tourists and art aficionados from all over the world are very fond of making a quick detour from the A8 highway to visit the famous Frauenkirche church in Günzburg, which was decorated by Dominikus Zimmermann. The Rococo structure is regarded as the predecessor of the famous Wies church. Even more interest is being generated at present, however, by the world's fourth Lego Park, located just outside the town.

Legoland, built from 4 million tiny plastic bricks, was opened in May 2002, and achieved respectable visitor figures of 1.3 million in its first season alone.

Erich Pawlu

The Ulmer Winkel

»Between the Iller and the Günz lies a peaceful and happy piece of land, with undulating hills, some high and wavy, others flatter and more gentle as they flow down into the plain. Dark-eyed forests stretch for miles to the horizon, rising and falling ...« During a search for the baroque in Swabia, art historian Herbert Schindler once wrote these words to describe the idyllic region known as the Ulmer Winkel.

Poetry has always been rather over-forgiving of reality. The district of Neu-Ulm with its 17 parishes (including those of Neu-Ulm and the towns of Senden, Vöhringen, Weissenhorn and Illertissen), located in the strip of land between the Danube and the Iller and known as the Ulmer Winkel, is actually a highly urban and industrialised area. Although it is one of the smallest districts in Bavaria in terms of surface area (it covers a mere 515.6 square kilometres), its 160,000 citizens give it the second-largest population in Bavarian Swabia – making it anything but a peaceful paradise for hermits wishing to get away from it all.

Innovative region, science park, Edison Centre, TFU Technology Promotion, Illertal Viererbande. When the district of Neu-Ulm gets discussed, its industrial achievements (such as its amount of GDP, or its rate of taxable capacity which puts it tenth in Bavaria) usually come top of the list. Ask anyone wearing traditional German dress in Neu-Ulm what they like best about their district and there will usually be a malicious reference either to the view of the filigree Gothic cathedral, the Ulmer Münster, on permanent loan from the Württembergers to their junior partner in Bavaria, or to the pointed roofs and gables of the old houses in the former Fishing Quarter. In other words, the best thing about Neu-Ulm is its view of Ulm. So is the district of Neu-Ulm a place entirely devoid of cultural interest?

It takes time to do a thing well. It certainly took time for the town of Neu-Ulm, a »forceps delivery« courtesy of Napoleon Bonaparte in 1810, to switch from being an anaemic border town with the name »Ulm on the right-hand bank of the Danube« to becoming a nice, healthy town in its own right. To attract settlers to the dirt-encrusted little community on the Bavarian bank of the Danube, King Max Joseph I decided to introduce tax breaks: anyone who built a house in Neu-Ulm would be freed of housing tax for five years, and anyone who drained and cultivated any of the surrounding moorland would be exempt from countryside tax for a full 10 years. The article in the Augsburg Postzeitung on June 5, 1867 was like music to the ears of the Neu-Ulmers: »In a few years' time, because of its location at the junction of four railway lines, two of them through Bavaria and two through Württemberg, Neu-Ulm will be one of the finest and busiest towns in Bavaria.«

The senior members of the rural community asked King Ludwig II most humbly to include them in the list of towns. On September 29, 1869, delighted by the small border town's steady rise to fame and fortune, the king conferred municipal status on it. In 1891 the administrative

Pages 36/37: The Ulmer Winkel, the stretch of land between the rivers Danube and Iller, is named after the former free imperial city of Ulm (its famous »Fischerviertel«, or Fishing Quarter, is shown here).
Top left: The Ulm Adlerbastei fortress, from which A. L. Berblinger, known as the »Tailor of Ulm«, made his unsuccessful escape in 1811.
Centre left, below left: Atmospheric shots of the famous Fishing Quarter in Ulm.

town with its garrison received the right to administer itself as a district of its own – and naturally lost it again after the local government reorganisation of 1972. To make up for this, the population of Neu-Ulm was increased by 14,000 and its surface area doubled to cover an area of 80 square kilometres.

Today, 130 years on, this town is anything but sleepy and provincial. Nor are its neighbours in the district either: Illertissen, Senden, Föhringen and Weissenhorn. Ever since the mid-19th century, when talented entrepreneurs used the waters of the Iller to run weaving businesses and metal rolling mills, this region has undergone a breathtaking development that has made it one of the most densely-populated in Bavaria with over 300 people per square kilometre.

The town of Neu-Ulm is on the verge of yet another development, too. When (as envisioned by the »Neu-Ulm 21« programme) the railway lines running through the town have been lowered, the old town centre and the southern part of the town (gradually developing on the area formerly covered by the American Wiley Barracks) will be able to grow together. The Regional Garden Show in 2008 will then mark the realization of a vision that will fill the area between the Südstadt and the suburb of Ludwigsfeld with leafy parks and green areas. Just the place to relax on a park bench under a blue sky during the summer ..

But the luxury of taking time out can of course already be detected today in the Ulmer Winkel: almost all the parishes have at least one horse-chestnut-tree covered beer garden where time can be whiled away. Since the landscape of this region is not exactly mountainous, indeed devastatingly flat, exploring it by bicycle is highly recommended – along the well-surfaced cycle paths beside the Danube and Iller rivers, for instance. Do so, and the art, culture and natural beauty of the region will become immediately obvious.

Those natural beauties were just as popular with the Roman gods, who swam at favourite locations by the Danube and sunned themselves in the meadows beside the Iller. One of them, the river god Danuvius, turns up each year with his colourful retinue for the »Nabada«. The Nabada can best be described as a convoy of anything that floats, and it heads down the Danube every year, on a Monday in July. Thousands of onlookers line the banks to watch carnival floats and other contraptions braving the waves. The Leonhardiritt, or »St. Leonard's Ride« in Weissenhorn, is similarly magnificent, as is the »Leiberprozession« in Roggenburg on August 15 each year – a commemoration of the time of religious confusion before the Catholic Church found its feet again.

Roggenburg is just the place to forget all about the monotony of urban life, in fact. Find yourself, and enjoy nature, too, with a trip to Roggenburg Monastery. Up to 200 years ago it was still the religious centre of a state covering 50 square kilometres, and today it has been brought back to life. Premonstratensian monks returned here in 1982, and the monastery has now become an

Above right: The »Blaue Traube« in Obenhausen.
Centre: The gatehouse in Illereichen. The European Women's Forum was started in this idyllic town in 1999.
Below: Entrance to the Fugger town of Weissenhorn with its massive Oberes Tor gate, the new town hall, and the Waaghaus to the north of it.

education centre for family, environment and culture. The main hall here is very impressive. The master builder Simpert Kraemer from Edelstetten truly reveals his talent for sensitive and playful architecture and design here in Roggenburg – even more so than in Ottobeuren, where he built the famous basilica plus palace-like monastery. Responding elegantly to the rhythm of its setting on a wooded rise above the Biber valley, the monastery church radiates solemn grandeur and joyful composure.

When the sun is shining, a boat trip on the lake beside the former monastery is a fine way of rounding off any visit. Swimming to get rid of muscle cramps is best left to health freaks – the autumn temperatures can be very bracing. A good place to take advantage of water's therapeutic properties, however, is the thermal bath at the »Atlantis« in Neu-Ulm, South Germany's most modern bathing centre. The thermal water bubbles up from 1000 metres below ground here, and the computer can generate 21 different kinds of wave across the pool.

Another very good place to loosen up and stretch your muscles is of course the »Nautilla« in Illertissen, assuming your nerves can cope with the unpleasant buzzing of insects around these former gravel pits that have now been filled with water for swimmers. The castle at Illertissen is also a good place to visit. The property of Memmingen patricians, the Vöhlin family, it contains a folk museum that since 1983 has also included a »bee museum«, complete with its own apis mellifica (Queen bee). The parish church of St. Martin is also worth a visit: a monument to the Renaissance spirit, it has an altar covered with fine sculpture by the Neuburg artist Christoph Rodt. The entire work is over eleven metres high, with music-making angels at the very top forming a »welcoming committee« for a pyramidal group of figures rising upward.

Above: Awoken from its enchanted sleep: Roggenburg Monastery.
Centre: The monastery library.
Below: A monument to the spirit of the Renaissance: Christoph Rodt's altar in Illertissen's parish church of St. Martin.

Sometimes it's nice to replace all those calories that get lost while cycling – and even though the smell of chips can be all-pervasive here as well, village inns do still exist. The food is traditional and delicious, with noodles (Spätzle) and fried onion accompanying roasts, or pancakes cut into thin strips and served in broth (Flädlesuppe). In some of these inns, notably in Biberach and Messhofen, beer specialities are on offer from young brewers. Deciding between a sensible shandy or a delicious mug of real ale is often rather difficult!

Inns like these have a reputation for being cosy, social places – especially between November and February each year when they are transformed into theatres. The halls resound with audience laughter during amateur dramatic performances in which the local farmer's wife seduces a whole series of men, the local postman becomes a dowry-hunter and the priest whispers oaths of love. These events are becoming extremely popular: why else would Weissenhorn's Catholic association have built a miniature theatre with fine neoclassical decoration in the attic of a fire station in 1876? The sight of the curtain opening there on a comic baroque opera is a superb experience for all theatre fans ...

Visiting Weissenhorn itself, however, is also a treat for the eye. Its centre – an oval area surrounded by fortifications, and measuring just 300 by 175 metres – contains two castles, a church, a town hall, the theatre mentioned above and also a whole series of picturesque patrician houses. At the entrance to the centre is a massive gate-tower with two round smaller ones in front of it. The Expressionist fresco on the gate is famous: painted by the Weissenhorn artist Anton Bischof (1877–1962) it commemorates the 12,000 furious farmers who marched to the gate here in April 1, 1525. The gate tower today contains the town's folk museum, and there are numerous valuable exhibits here – including, amazingly enough, four oriental heads by the Venetian artist Giovanni Battista Tiepolo.

The Ulmer Winkel has a vast number of museums. For Asterix fans, for instance, the »Neu-Ulm museums on the Petrusplatz« are an absolute must: in the prehistoric collection here you can find magnificent harnesses, a clay mug and a leg of lamb from a burial mound near Illerberg; they were placed alongside a Celtic prince for his journey into the beyond. In the room next door there are sculptures and paintings by Neu-Ulm native Edwin Scharff, a contemporary of Lehmbruck, Barlach and Kolbe.

In 1999 Neu-Ulm gave its local artists an attractive »Fine Arts Museum«, housed in the former brewery in Oberfahlheim, a late baroque gem with a two-storey gable. Inside, local painters can exhibit their work, and a visit here can often be a real eye-opener, proving that provincial art is anything but tedious and predictable.

At 7.30 am on Monday, October 14, 1805, Father Benedikt Baader, archivist of the monastery in Oberelchingen, sat down at his diary and made the following entry: »Like a black thundercloud announcing imminent lightning and hail, the French armies have entered the streets of Ulm, Steinheim, Strass and Fahlheim and adopted battle formation.« It was not long before the French spearhead, in its blue-and-white uniforms, marched against the Austrian army, forcing it slowly back up the monastery hill in a hail of bullets. Several cannonballs also landed in the church of the former Benedictine monastery. When the victorious Napoleon visited the church on the morning of October 16, 1805, he was overwhelmed by the magnificence of its white-and-gold neoclassical interior: »C'est vraiment le salon du Bon Dieu!«

At that time the »Lord's living room« was already the property of the elector of Bavaria; Napoleon had given it to him to compensate for the loss of the regions on the left bank of the Rhine. The sudden end of the Holy Roman Empire not only spelt the end for the Benedictine monastery of Elchingen, however, but also for the Premonstratensians in Roggenburg. Now a kingdom, Bavaria soon had a say in the control of the various sections of the political jigsaw acquired by the Habsburgs as well as Ulm's former imperial territory on the right bank of the Danube. It took a long time for Neu-Ulm and its district to become self-confident partners of Ulm itself.

Eduard Ohm

Facing page: White and gold magnificence: the parish church of Peter and Paul and the former Benedictine monastery in Oberelchingen.
Right, above: The elegant castle in the Neu-Ulm district of Hausen.
Centre: A Gothic country church of great rarity – St. Margareta in Reutti.
Below: The Vöhlin castle in Illertissen overlooks the town and the entire Iller valley.
Photos pp. 39/41/43 courtesy of Designstudio Bauer, Neu-Ulm.

Central Swabia

Does Central Swabia actually exist? And if so, where is it? Northern Swabia has the Ries, and Southern Swabia has the Allgäu, but where exactly is Central Swabia?

Explaining to the unfamiliar that Swabia exists not only in Württemberg but also between the Iller and Lech rivers is already difficult enough. Yet even the locals themselves find it hard to define exactly where the centre of Swabia lies. There are three Swabian regions – Augsburg, Donau-Iller and Allgäu – and district names such as Dillingen, Neu-Ulm, Günzburg and Unter-Allgäu, but these are not much of a help either. As an administrative area, Central Swabia does not exist, so the best way to define it is probably by describing what it is not. Dillingen and the Donau-Ries belong to the north, Neu-Ulm lies to the west, the Unterallgäu takes up the south of Swabia, and Augsburg and the district of the same name are more a part of eastern Swabia, not least because of their social and economic ties with Aichach and Friedberg. Then again, people from that region would never describe themselves as Eastern Swabians.

What remains after all the rest has been subtracted is basically the district of Günzburg, or at least its southern section. For decades Günzburg hosted the »Northern Swabia Exhibition«, while Krumbach – which confidently styles itself »the heart of Central Swabia« – is the home of the local newspaper known as the Mittelschwäbische Nachrichten (Central Swabian News, one of the local editions of the Augsburger Allgemeine). Even after the local government reorganisation of 1972, this newspaper has made frequent mention of the Altlandkreis Krumbach, or »former district of Krumbach«, with reference to the former seat of the district administration. Here, therefore, and also in Neuburg an der Kammel, both of them located in the former district of Krumbach, we can safely say we are on Central Swabian terrain. Does this also apply to the northern part of today's district of Günzburg? Let's find out: the market town of Jettingen-Scheppach (close to the famous church of Allerheiligen) describes its municipal area as »the centre of Bavarian Swabia«. So that would put Wetterhausen, located on the same line of latitude, firmly at the heart of Swabia too. Whether official or not, Central Swabia, with all its sights and attractions, is a delightful, historic landscape that not only has numerous treasures but is also very fond of presenting them to their best advantage.

Title picture: The interior of the parish church of St. Michael in Krumbach, one of the main works of Simpert and Johann Martin Kraemer.
Facing page: The parish church of St. Michael, dominating the centre of Krumbach.
Below: The Krumbad has made an excellent name for itself as a health spa, and the surrounding forests contain some magnificent walks.

Krumbach

Anyone approaching this town from the north will immediately be struck by its beautiful location in an open valley, and by the sight of all the picturesque rooftops and towers in the distance. Even though the road first has to pass the usual industrial and trading areas, it soon enters the charming town itself. Krumbach received its municipal charter in 1895, and the anniversary in 1995 was very happily celebrated. There was less enthusiasm in 1972, however, when the local government reorganisation shifted the district administration, tax office and law courts to neighbouring Günzburg.

Since that time the Bavarian Free State has tried to make amends for the local government reorganisation by moving the water administration and regional police headquarters here. Krumbach's loss of importance has been compounded by its unfavourable location from the traffic point of view: there has been a constant battle to retain the single-track rail connection to Günzburg and Mindelheim, and the A7, A8 and A96 highways, all of which have exits marked Krumbach, are all 25 kilometres away from the place.

This former market town of Vorderoesterreich has managed to preserve its independence, however. It is still a busy place, functioning as the heart of a largely rural region whose population are happy to work, shop and relax in the former district town. The town centre is an especially lively place, and is characterised by such landmarks as the parish church of St. Michael (one of the major works of Simpert and Johann Martin Kraemer), the neighbouring castle (built in the early 16th century under imperial councillor Hans Lamparter von Greiffenstein), and the market square with its historic town hall. Built in 1679, the latter stands proudly at the centre of a square lined by magnificent townhouses.

The museum and the Jewish Cemetery are reminders of the time when Krumbach was home to a significantly large Jewish community. The Chapel of St. Mary in the cemetery with the large-format Christmas painting by Konrad Huber underlines Krumbach's importance as a centre of Old Swabian nativity scene models.

The moated castle of Hürben also strengthens the impression of a leafy town, as does the nearby Krumbad, famous as a health spa and also ideal for long walks through beautiful forests.

All in all, Krumbach is a small and appealing town that has no need to seek a role of its own. Finding one's way around is easy, and the flair of the place attracts many tourists. This is where to find Central Swabia.

Neuburg an der Kammel

If the best view of Krumbach is from on high, with the town nestling in its valley, the opposite applies where Neuburg is concerned: the gate-tower and main structure of Vöhlin Castle tend to make the visitor look upward. This castle, built in the Renaissance style in 1567, was a residence of the wealthy Vöhlin family of merchants from Memmingen. A lime-tree-lined avenue leads to the castle courtyard, where visitors can then enter the lovingly restored rooms of the castle which is now a hotel and restaurant. Once owned by the state and then by Freiherr von Arentin, the castle was purchased by Peter Baumann, a businessman from Gundelfingen, in 1998. Music, dancing, family celebrations and markets have all given the castle and the surrounding area a new lease of life.

Walking down from the castle area into the town below is highly worthwhile for several reasons. The artistically inclined will enjoy a rare Deposition sculpture in the parish church of Maria Himmelfahrt. It is the work of this market town's greatest son, the gifted sculptor Christoph Rodt (1578–1634), who is commemorated by a plaque on a half-timbered façade below the church. Rodt's sculpture group, which consists of individual figures forming a scenic whole, can be observed and appreciated from several different angles.

Neuburg's neighbouring town of Edelstetten became a part of it in 1978. Edelstetten Castle, a three-storey collegiate building with an inner courtyard, was built between 1682 and 1705. It is currently being renovated with public funds. The magnificent church is one of the main works of Edelstetten master builder Simpert Kraemer. The monastery complex is owned by the princes of Esterházy, who have welcomed the idea of it housing the Swabian Literature Archive. The Archive has brought the castle, with its picturesque Chinoiserie-decorated main hall, back into the limelight with a series of public

Above: The Renaissance castle of Neuburg an der Kammel has been given a new lease of life. Facing page: Floral displays outside windows testify to the pride of local inhabitants in their town.

events, especially the Bavarian-Swabian Literature Awards ceremony and the »Storytelling for Students« competition. Together with its interesting castle chapel, this monastery complex is well on its way to becoming a further attraction of Neuburg.

Wettenhausen

The Chinese Hall in Edelstetten may still be largely undiscovered, but the Kaisersaal in Wettenhausen is famed far beyond the borders of its town. Many local people rather regret the fact that Wettenhausen became part of a larger group of towns collectively named Kammeltal as part of the local government reorganisation. Wettenhausen is, after all, outstanding from the point of view of art history. Its monastery, a magnificent Baroque building, is one of the gems of Central Swabia. The onion domes of the monastery church, built in 1612, are an integral part of the fine blend between culture and landscape that is so typical of this region's architecture. Originally founded in the 12th century as an Augustinian monastery, today the building is a Dominican convent, and it also houses a grammar school run by the diocese of Augsburg. The monastery complex of Wettenhausen is the most impressive in all of Central Swabia.

The church and the monastery form a harmonious whole, and are enhanced still further by the art of the stucco plasterers of Wessobrunn. Today's school hall, filled with stucco and frescoes in 1694 as the monastery's first Kaisersaal, contains 10 fine fresco allegories, wall-to-wall acanthus-leaf decoration containing 11 medallions, and numerous angels around its main

picture. It all bears witness to astonishingly creative artwork, glorifying the House of Habsburg with stylistic brilliance and formal variety. The entire room emanates perfect harmony in its size, dimensions and carefully-placed decoration. Form, light and colour combine to create a Gesamtkunstwerk, a breathtaking architectural and artistic achievement.

The stuccowork was added to the Kaisersaal in 1694 by Hans Jörg Brix from Günzburg. The identity of the artist who created the over-lifesized angel figures is unfortunately unknown, while the 11 frescoes glorifying the House of Habsburg were the work of Paul Etschmann from Wiblingen. After secularization, and later on during World War II, the hall lost much of its splendour. From 1964 to 1965, however, it was restored to its former glory as part of the centenary celebrations for the Dominican convent in Wettenhausen.

Allerheiligen

The magnificent church of Allerheiligen (All Saints) makes it clear that the northern region of Günzburg also belongs to the so-called schwäbische Barockwinkel, or »Swabian Baroque area«, a term coined in a thesis about tourism in the region by the student Claudia Jah from Offingen. The name can now be read on the brown-and-white traffic signs for tourists along the A 8 highway.

If you arrive at the foot of the »holy mountain« from Scheppach, one of the municipalities that make up the market town of Jettingen-Scheppach, there are still over 100 steps to climb before you reach the forested and formerly fortified plateau above, and can enjoy the view far across the surrounding landscape. Facing you is the nave of a Rococo-style church, with a tower at the southern end. A small hermitage is located on its northern side, and around the base of the tower is a twostorey seminary, which also contains the sacristy and, on its upper floor, an oratory for the choir.

The nave was built between 1731 and 1732 by Simpert Kraemer from Edelstetten. Broad pilasters with plinths, bases and capitals line the outer wall, which is broken up by four round-arched windows.

The choir section of Allerheiligen was an innovative early work by Joseph Dossenberger, and is thought to have been built between 1753 and 1755. The master builder of Wettenhausen adopted Dominikus Zimmermann's motif of the convex outer wall, which lends additional power to the characteristic ground-plan of the choir by emphasising its centre. The frescoes on the ceilings and projecting galleries, 26 of them in all, are among the most important works by Johann Baptist Enderle, and the themes range from Adoration of the Magi to renditions of Jesus as a young boy. The pilgrimage church of Allerheiligen is one of the cultural gems of Central Swabia, and famed far beyond the region. From the 14th century onwards, the church built here at this place of pilgrimage has been visible for miles around, and for decades now has attracted visitors from near and far for the Swabian Mariensingen event held on the last Sunday of September. Popular piety and high culture combine here to create an inseparable harmony.

Facing page: Wettenhausen, today a Dominican convent, still dominates the view of the Kammel Valley.
Above: Tree-lined streets are a common feature of the towns in Central Swabia, and harmonise with the well-tended houses.

Any visit to the church is best followed by a meal in the inn next door to it. Jakob Seiter, the innkeeper, carries on a 125-year family tradition by playing the zither to his guests and inviting them to sing along. The delicious homemade delicacies include game, and many sunny days are happily spent here in the shade of the horse-chestnut trees (also 125 years old).

Allerheiligen and numerous other places in this region make it clear that even though the delightful landscape here lacks the sheer variety of other parts of Swabia, the basic values here have lasted for centuries and are as meaningful as ever to the local population. The artwork is of high quality yet unpretentious, the people's piety is simple and unaffected, and even though they feel closely bound to their region, they never seal themselves off from outside. This region is provincial in the very best sense of the word, with its open and welcoming lifestyle, its calm and self-confident acceptance of its own roots.

Rudolf Köppler

AUGSBURG

SWIMMING IN LAKES AND RIVERS

In the pale summer, when the winds above
Whistle only through the leaves of the big trees
Is the time to lie in rivers or ponds
Like the plants where pikes lurk.
Your body grows light in the water. If your arm
Happens to fall gently from the water into the sky
The gentle breeze sways it forgetfully
Having probably mistaken it for a brown branch.

The sky at noon is vast and silent.
You close your eyes when swallows come.
The mud is warm. If cool bubbles appear
You know that a fish has just swum between us.
My body, my thigh and the stationary arm
Lie still in the water, fully united
And only when the cool fish swim through us
Do I feel that the sun is shining above the pond ...

Bertolt Brecht

A lot has been written about Bertolt Brecht's difficult relationship with Augsburg. And yet in Brecht's early poetry, one senses a deep affinity and reconciliation with the place. As much water flows through his youthful poems as it does through the famous city. In Augsburg it is the rivers Wertach and Lech, which eventually join each other north of the old city in the wilderness known as the Wolfzahnau. These are the Lech meadows, the jungles and ponds along the shingle-filled banks of the green river, where losing your bearings between the water and the sky is comparatively easy.

This water also feeds the numerous canals that rush through the city from south to north. Thanks to the generosity of the city to its inhabitants, stretches of them have been equipped with ladders for climbing and beach sections for sunbathing, so you can let yourself float along or, depending on your mood, swim against the current. The Eiskanal even made Olympic history in 1972 when the canoeing championships were held there. The historic waterworks are also located on the Eiskanal, a masterpiece of late 19th-century architecture proving (just like the building in the Wolfzahnau with its magnificent tiled arches) that the power of water has continually inspired the people of Augsburg to produce innovative technology and first-class architecture. The Hochablass weir, with its pretty little pointed green towers, channels the power of the Lech across the full width of the river. Up on the walkway, people are amazed to see the gentle

Previous page: The Augustus Fountain, the first of Augsburg's magnificent fountains, modelled by Hubert Gerhard in 1594, stands opposite the Town Hall, which was built between 1615 and 1620 by Elias Holl. Above: The Hercules Fountain, designed by Adriaen de Vries, with a view of the Church of St. Ulrich. Below: To celebrate the 2000-year anniversary of the city in 1985, the Town Hall's famous Goldener Saal, destroyed during a bombing raid in 1944, was reconstructed according to old plans.

river arrive from the south, with its ducks and swans, and then turn into the thundering chaos beneath their feet. Those lying safely in the sunshine on the gravel banks a little farther away can shudder quietly as they enjoy the distant roaring sound.

Water is omnipresent in the heart of the city, too. Down in the Lech Quarter, the canals (Vorderer, Mittlerer and Hinterer Lech) have been uncovered again by intelligent civic engineers. From the Middle Ages onwards they provided the power for craftsmen as well as sweeping away their rubbish, and today they bubble away as fresh as ever beneath the countless bridges, giving the old part of town no chance to become a dried-up and ancient museum. Water also rushes past the house where Brecht was born, at Auf dem Rain 7, which can only be reached via a small footbridge. It is said that Augsburg has more bridges than Venice. Water also dominates the streets higher up – the famous Maximilianstrasse, for instance, where it has been artistically concentrated into three magnificent fountains. The statues of Augustus, Mercury and Hercules gain a special and generous lightness beyond the play of water, and when the famous Föhn (sudden warm and sunny weather from Italy) crosses the Alps and lights up the historic facades, or when the full moon lights up Maximilianstrasse from behind St. Ulrich and the young people gather around the Hercules statue with their wineglasses, intensely aware of the energy of the place, the city of

Above: The symbol of trade, the bronze statue of Mercury, messenger of the gods, designed by Adriaen de Vries in 1599 and cast by Wolfgang Neidhart. The Weberhaus can be seen in the background. Below: The most impressive rococo structure in Augsburg is the Schaezler Palais. Today it houses the German Baroque Gallery and the Municipal Art Gallery. The masterpiece is the 23-metre-long ballroom with its ceiling frescoes by Gregorio Guglielmi.

Augsburg becomes something that cannot have left even Brecht cold.

Augsburg is a city with a great history, and water played a very important role in it. Shortly before Christ's birth the Romans set up a military encampment at the confluence of the Lech and Wertach rivers, which soon developed into the centre of the new imperial province of Rhaetia and was known as Augusta Vindelicum. The main trading route to Italy at that time was the Via Claudia Augusta. On the high ridge separating the two rivers, protected by the Alpine floods, the episcopal city was born – Augsburg Cathedral stands at one end of that ridge today with the merchant quarter to the south of it, and the other end of the ridge is marked by the church of St. Ulrich and Afra. Bishop Ulrich (symbolised by a fish) defended the city against Hungarian invasion on the Lech Plain in the year 955.

Augsburg was one of the first medieval cities to provide a drinking-water system for its inhabitants. In 1804, on a visit to Augsburg, the poet August von Kotzebue was astonished at »the magnificent art by which so many houses and streams are provided with such a plentiful supply of water ... Just as quickly as tiny thoughts are pumped through tiny veins to the brain by God and then stream into the world via sheets of paper, the water here is gathered four storeys high in large containers and then channelled into people's houses through thousands of tiny pipes. The people then have the choice of using the supply or of simply

Thanks to old documents, the history of the Cathedral can be reconstructed back to the year 823. The oldest section is probably the crypt under the west choir, built under Bishop Ulrich in the 10th century. There are frescoes from the Romanesque and Gothic periods, fine vault paintings and four portraits by Hans Holbein the Elder. The four »prophet windows«, portraying Jonas, Daniel, Hosea and Moses, probably date from the 12th century and are among the earliest of their type in Germany. Below: The cloister, with its ancient sepulchral slabs, dates from the 15th century.

allowing it to continue flowing by.« It should be noted that today the city still has an excellent supply of drinking water from the nearby Siebentisch Forest, and carefully ensures that it remains pure.

The Via Claudia, the trading route from north to south, caused trade to flourish, and the Lech canals helped craft businesses to prosper. One such was weaving, which enabled the craft's most famous exponents, the Fugger family, to achieve international fame and fortune. They decided the election of Emperor Karl V in 1519, and had a vast influence on imperial politics – while lining their own pockets in the process, of course. To compensate for their success they commissioned the world's first ever council estate for the poor, the Fuggerei, which is still run today in the spirit of its founders.

At the beginning of the modern age, Augsburg was the political and artistic centre of Europe, the town of the Reformation and the Renaissance. This is where the great ecumenical debates were held, and the church and convent of St. Anna played a major role (Luther stayed there in 1518 to defend his theses against Kajetan). It was in Augsburg that the Confessio Augustana was proclaimed at the Reichstag of 1530, and the Peace of Augsburg sealed in 1555. A few decades later the magnificent fountains were built in the Maximilianstrasse, and the water towers at the Rotes Tor, or Red Gate, were supplied with water by the city's brilliant architect Elias Holl. This masterly technical achievement went hand in

Above: The Goldsmiths' Chapel of the Lutheran Protestant church of St. Anna, formerly the church of a Carmelite monastery, contains carefully restored Late Gothic frescoes.
Centre: A view of the northern transept of the Catholic church of St. Ulrich.
Below: The Late Gothic basilica, with valuable Renaissance and baroque decoration, contains the tombs of canonized bishops Afra, Ulrich and Simpert.

hand with a cultural one: the fountains were an expression of how proud the city was of the way it had harnessed water to its needs. The statue of Augustus in the Town Hall Square was surrounded by statues symbolising the Augsburg rivers – the Lech, Wertach, Singold and Brunnenlech – whose combined power guaranteed prosperity and quality of life. This was appreciated by Queen Christine of Sweden in 1655 when she wrote: »Augsburg is one of the most beautiful, most noble and most famous cities in Germany, situated in a very graceful and well-irrigated plain, whereby the soil is most fertile.«

When he rebuilt the city's Town Hall opposite the Augustus Fountain, Elias Holl brought Italy straight to Augsburg. Still elated by his experiences in the lagoon city of Venice, he gave the free imperial city of Augsburg a »beautiful, new and well-proportioned« work of great clarity, the most important secular Renaissance building in Germany: the Town Hall. Light still falls through its 60 generously spaced windows and into the Goldener Saal, the magnificent chamber inside. After the building was destroyed by bombs in February 1944, reconstruction of the Town Hall to its former glory became a top priority for all of Augsburg's citizens. The Perlach Tower, beside the Town Hall, dominates the square like an Italian campanile, turning the platz into a piazza.

The city fortifications, which were also partly the work of Elias

The Fuggerei is the oldest housing estate in the world. It was religious motives that prompted Jakob Fugger »the Rich« and his brothers Ulrich and Georg to found this settlement for burghers who had become impoverished through no fault of their own. The medieval concept of doing good in order to go to Heaven probably played a major role, as did the new Humanism deriving from the Renaissance. Construction work began in 1516, and the 52 houses were completed in 1523.

Holl, formed the basis for the water idylls that are a special feature of Augsburg today: the water flows through am Graben, then past the magnificent horse-chestnut trees at the Rotes Tor gate, then past the Vogeltor gate, the Barfuesser Bridge, the Liliom and the Fünffinger Tower, until it reaches the meadows and tree-lined banks near the Oblatterwall, very close to where Brecht was born. The cultural historian Wilhelm Heinrich Riehl, writing in the mid-19th century, noticed that the city fortifications were far more romantic than martial, and mentioned »the semi-dilapidated city wall ... with its mighty stone bridges and waterways, the secret dark waters of the Stadtgraben near the fountain of Emperor Maximilian, and the attractive areas of water beside the Jakober and Oblatter Gates«. He continued: »This is no modern, artificial Romanticism, but an ancient one that tells us of the city's history and its character. The centuries-old avenues of lime trees and horse-chestnut trees along the walls show us how peaceful even the old Augsburgers intended their fortifications to be. Ever since the 16th century, deer have grazed in the upper moat areas, swans have swum across the clear waters below the walls of the lower town, and the finest truffles can be sought and found under the lawns beside the city walls.«

The majestic side of Augsburg is nowhere more evident than in the famous Rococo Hall inside the city's Schaezler Palais, which forms a fine backdrop to the Hercules Fountain in Maximilian-

Each house in the Fuggerei was given a garden, so that the families could plant their own vegetables and be largely self-sufficient. They were also given an apartment of their own with everything they needed, even cutlery.
»Be needy, but in dignity« was the motto, and the occupants earned the annual rent money of one guilder by praying three times to their founders and benefactors.

strasse. The wealth required to produce such magnificent architecture derived not only from the skill of this family of gold- and silversmiths, but also from the genius of their bankers; the cultural expression, however, resulted from the fact that the architect of this palace, Freiherr Liebert von Liebenhofen, and his son-in-law Friedrich von Schaezler, had been elevated to the ranks of the nobility. The ball held at the official opening of the hall in 1770 was attended by no less a person than Marie-Antoinette – an event that Augsburg never forgets to remind its visitors about, even today. The daughter of Emperor Franz I was probably most impressed by the dimensions of the Maximilianstrasse and the suitable backdrop it provided with its three fountains, despite the fact that the middle one, the Mercury Fountain, self-confidently revealed Augsburg's identity as a merchants' city.

In the year 1784, the monk Johann Nepomuk Hauntinger collected his impressions in a travel journal as follows: »We passed by noisy canals and moss-covered banks until we reached the Red Gate and entered beautiful Augsburg, which had already provided some spectacular views from afar. The fact that Augsburg is the finest and largest city in Swabia is well-known, especially to the Augsburgers themselves. It is not as populated as Munich, although it covers a larger area. The main street from St. Ulrich to the Town Hall is lined by the finest of town houses, and is as broad and as majestic as any such thoroughfare in Munich.«

Above: The ensemble making up the Rotes Tor and the Heilig-Geist-Spital bears the unmistakable stamp of architect Elias Holl.
Centre left: Open canals, small bridges and old craftsmen's houses give the Lech quarter its special flair. Centre right: According to legend, the »Stone Man« statue commemorates a baker named Hacker, who waved a large loaf from the city wall during a siege in 1635 to demonstrate the townspeople's defiance.
Below: Boat trips along the Oblatterwall.

Here once can already sense something that would gradually become a trauma for the people of Augsburg: their city's rivalry with Munich. The wound was inflicted in 1806, when Augsburg's days as a free imperial city were ended by Napoleon and it was given to the kingdom of Bavaria. Ever since that time, if some opinions are to be believed, the city's pride has been shattered, and it has never been able to come to terms with what happened. Nevertheless, the 19th century was a period of prosperity for the city, especially as far as industrialisation was concerned. The Haindl paper factory was founded, the foundations of the famous firm of MAN (Maschinenfabrik Augsburg-Nürnberg) were laid, Rudolf Diesel invented his famous engine, and the products of the Augsburg textile industry were in great demand all over Europe. Here, too, the waters of the river Lech played a decisive role. The textile quarter arose in the canal-filled area between the city wall and the Lech; water, in the age of the steam engine, provided a cheap source of energy. The canals are still a distinctive feature of the textile quarter. As in all the previous periods – the Roman era, the Middle Ages, the patrician era, and the Renaissance with its artists and town planners – the age of industrialisation also brought forth architecture of the highest quality. The Schülesche Calico Factory was built to look like a baroque castle, and first-class architects were brought to the textile quarter to build structures with important-sounding names: the Glaspalast (Glass Palace), for instance, or the

Below: The Jakober Gate was saved by a citizens' action group. The decision to pull down the 15th-century Gothic tower was made in 1876, but a majority of the populace then decided that the »picturesque object from a bygone age« should be preserved. As a compromise, the street to the south of the tower was widened slightly. This is where the famous »Dult« fair takes place twice yearly, between the Jakober and Vogel Gates.

Fabrikschloss (Factory Fortress). By the time the gasworks were built just before the First World War, the city had long since decided to commemorate its technological success with the construction of an outstanding ensemble of buildings. Augsburg is only just beginning to realize the importance of this stage of its history; the pain at the recent collapse of its textile industry, which nourished so many families for so long, is still there. This makes it all the more important, however, to gain a new awareness of the mute witnesses of that industrial heyday. The age of industrialisation changed the face of Augsburg radically, and has produced a unique and very attractive mixture of styles.

It was during that age that an architectural gem appeared just beyond the city gates: the Kurhaus Theatre in Göggingen. Glass, iron, palm-trees and plush furnishings combine here to form the elegant and slightly eccentric interior originally created by orthopaedic specialist Johann Friedrich von Hessing for his patients. Unfortunately this little theatre is still an »insider tip« and not as well-known as it should be, even though a great deal of public money was recently spent on its renovation.

Indeed, the city of Augsburg is an insider tip in itself. Those familiar with Augsburg as a sign on the Munich-Stuttgart motorway or as a stop on the railway line will be both surprised and delighted if they take a closer look at the city and the Swabian region surrounding it. There is nothing cute about

Above: A view of the outer stage of the Kurhaus Theatre in Göggingen, built in 1885.
Below: Cast iron and glass in the auditorium of the Kurhaus Theatre. The building reflects the opulent tastes of the man who commissioned it, Friedrich Hessing, and also of his architect Jean Keller. Using improvisation and trompe d'oeil, the French architect fulfilled the wishes of his master. This masterpiece of architectural engineering took just one year to build.

the place – despite the fame of the Augsburger Puppenkiste puppet theatre – and one sees none of the fruit orchards and museum-like half-timbered houses familiar from the Stuttgart region, nor any of the arrogant carnation-lined balconies of Upper Bavaria beyond Munich. Instead there is a noble and distinguished simplicity about the place, rooted in centuries of harmony between culture and landscape; an austere elegance that derives some of its presence from the unexpected and the unusual. Or perhaps we should say from a certain alienation – we are, after all, in the birthplace of dramatist Bertolt Brecht. The Protestant and Catholic St. Ulrich churches lean against each other like two unequal siblings. Villas stand beside factories, and the fine rococo hall in which Princess Marie Antoinette danced was built by a merchant. Along the horse-chestnut-lined moats of the old free imperial city, famed for its religious peace, one can hear a faint metallic sound – the sound of its factories, as distinctive as the famous rolled »r« sound in its dialect. The chimneys tower as high as the church steeples – and the water that drove the city's historical development also has several faces. It is not always friendly and helpful: during Whitsun in 1999, the river Wertach flooded entire districts, and no-one quite trusts it any more. Regardless of all its past ups and downs, Augsburg remains a living city, a city in perpetual flow – just like the water to which it owes its power and its beauty.

Eva Leipprand

Above: The Herz-Jesu Kirche is one of the finest churches of its time, and contains magnificent art nouveau decoration.
Centre: The former outhouses at the Cistercian convent of Oberschönenfeld contain the Swabian Folk Museum. The church, the convent and the inn form a magnificent ensemble at the heart of the Westliche Wälder forests outside Augsburg.
Below: Autumn scenery near Burgwalden.

Old Bavaria in Swabia

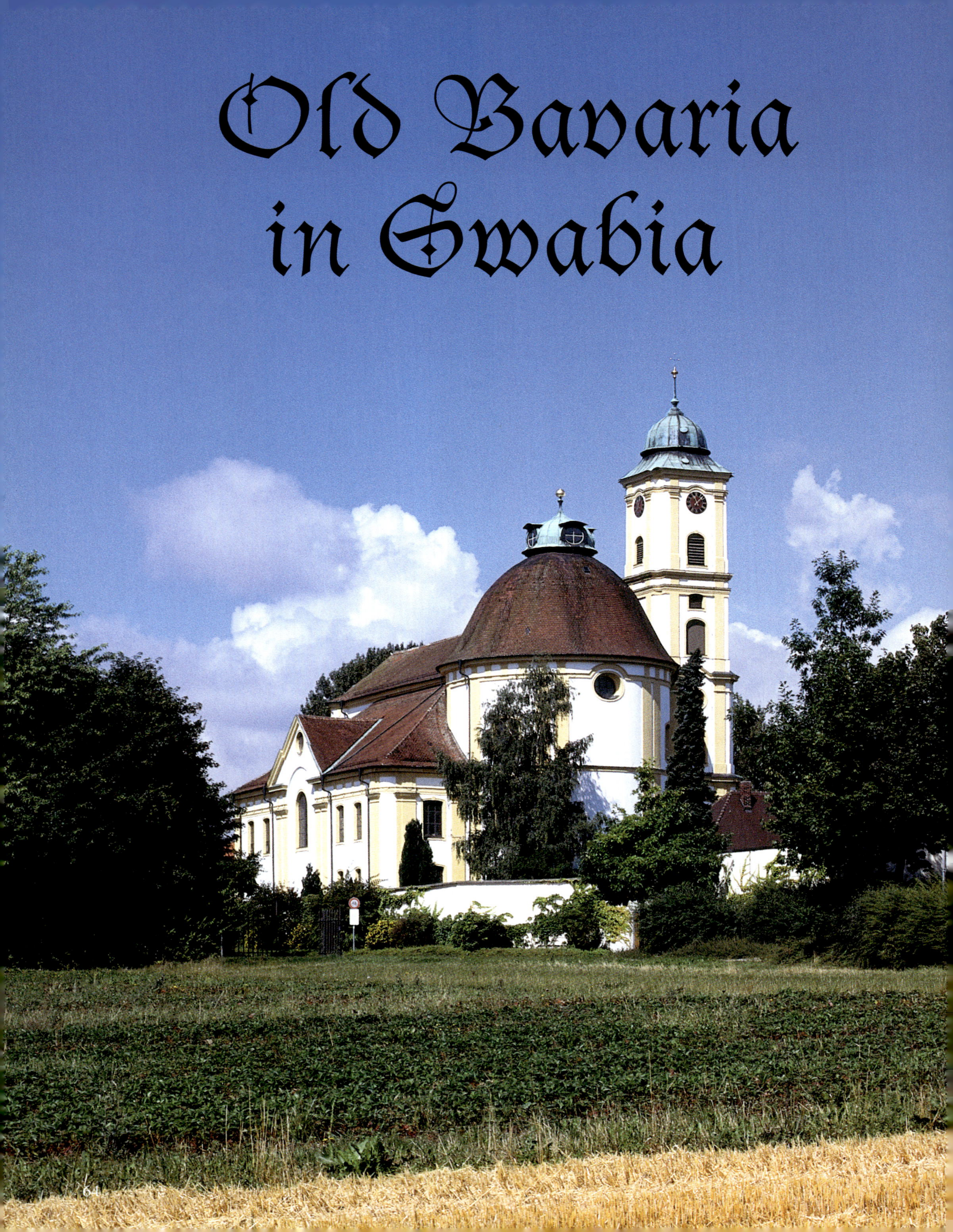

The Swabians were very lucky that the Altbayern, or Old Bavarians, have no Asterix or Obelix in their ranks – because otherwise they would have had just as little joy from the territory east of the river Lech that they won in 1972 as the Romans did in the province of Gaul. Over 30 years after the local government reorganisation, the wounds have certainly healed in the region of Aichach-Friedberg, but newspaper articles referring quite correctly to »Swabian« Aichach still trouble their readers there. The people of Friedberg have probably grown more accustomed to the idea of being Swabian rather than Bavarian now, even though their town, located high above the plain of the Lech river, was pillaged and destroyed by Swabian Augsburg on two occasions (in 1296 and 1372). Being »conquered« by Swabia back in 1944 was something of a surprise to the Friedbergers – but time heals all wounds, and Old Bavaria is still Old Bavaria, even though part of it now happens to lie in Swabia.

Yet what is so special about this eastern border region that places such importance on its Old Bavarian origins? It certainly has none of the picture-book and blatantly Bavarian attractions that tourists might expect. Here there are none of the spectacular mountain ranges and dazzling lakes with tiny villages so familiar from the Alpine foothills, indeed, nothing »typically Bavarian« at all. In the gently undulating hills beyond the towers of Friedberg there are indeed settlements nestling away in the cultural landscape with interesting architectural remains, towns with striking sights and also the odd fine church. But the roofs of the old buildings are just as steep as in neighbouring Swabia, the villages just as rigorously planned and the people just as reserved. There is, however, one important difference: the people here speak Bavarian, and think and feel that way as well.

Some Swabian-Alemannian speakers who settled long since in the green hills to the east of Augsburg still remain strongly aware of their dialect many years later. The inhabitants of this largely rural landscape are deeply rooted in Bavarian culture, and not necessarily all that keen on things Swabian. Even the small river Paar that crosses the landscape here gives the Lech a wide berth and heads for the Danube instead.

The most remarkable historical event on which today's region of Aichach-Friedberg can base its unique importance for Bavarian history happened in the year 1000. The Counts of Scheyern, ancestors of the Bavarian royal household, chose a small castle called Oberwittelsbach near Aichach as the centre of their realm, located at that time on the Paar between the Lech plain, Glonn and Donaumoos. They named themselves the Wittelsbacher, after the castle. Today the name of that noble household also stands for the region of Aichach-Friedberg.

On the outskirts of Friedberg, the Baroque pilgrimage church of Herrgottsruh (previous page, three photos above) towers above the surrounding countryside. The chapel of Maria Alber (below) stands close to the former tollbooth of the Dukes of Bavaria at the Augsburg town limits. Right: St. Mary's Fountain by the town hall in Friedberg.

The idea of referring to the region as »Wittelsbacher Land« in order to strengthen the sense of togetherness among Old Bavarians in Swabia is a new one. It was introduced as an »indication of place of origin« in 1999 for agricultural products. The corresponding logo, also on holiday brochures, has been quite successful ever since. Traffic signs along the highway between Stuttgart and Munich make it clear even to faster drivers that they are in the middle of Bavaria.

Nothing remains of the former castle. It is thought to have been destroyed in 1209 as an act of revenge for the murder of the Hohenstaufen King Philipp by Otto VIII, the last Count Palatine (the so-called »Regicide of Bamberg«). The castle square in Oberwittelsbach, which underwent archaeological investigation during the 800-year anniversary of the House of Wittelsbach in 1980, contains a Late Gothic church. Not far away from it, a neo-Gothic »National Monument« commemorates the proud era of the young kingdom of Bavaria at the beginning of the 19th century. It was financed by donations from the people of Bavaria and ceremonially unveiled before a large crowd of worthies on August 25th, 1834 – the birthday as well as name-day of King Ludwig I. His Majesty did not return in person to his family seat on this occasion, however; in those days, another member of the royal household visited »his Wittelsbach castle« far more often. Many newspaper articles of that time referred not to the sunken castle of Oberwittelsbach but to the idyllically situated, moated castle in nearby Unterwittelsbach. From 1838 it belonged to Duke Max of

Bavaria, father of the later Empress Elisabeth of Austria and Queen of Hungary. The zither-playing duke, who lived quite happily in Unterwittelsbach until 1850, was very popular with the common people yet has been long forgotten. His headstrong daughter Sisi, on the other hand, immortalised by the sentimental films starring Romy Schneider and Karlheinz Böhm as the Emperor Franz Joseph, is still very much of a crowd-puller. The regional capital of Aichach thus decided to turn the castle at Unterwittelsbach into a kind of memorial to her, rather than to her father. The year 2000 marked the beginning of a series of exhibitions in the »Sisi Castle«, all of them very popular with day trippers from the Augsburg region. Sceptics still cannot find conclusive proof that Sisi really did accompany her father to Unterwittelsbach now and then as a child. The anecdote about the young Elisabeth walking around with a hat to collect donations when Duke Max played the zither in the inns of Aichach does sound almost too good to be true, however.

Thanks to the magic wrought by Sisi, the small castle – which unfortunately contains no original furniture – is open to the public at intervals. Alongside the castle in Friedberg with its museum collection of valuable Friedberg watches and faience, and numerous items from prehistory, it is the only structure in the whole of Wittelsbacher Land that can also be admired from the inside. Around a dozen other castles – from Schorn, Pöttmes and Baar in the north, Mergenthau and Schmiechen in the south, Affing, Scherneck and Pichl in the west and Blumenthal, Kühbach, Rapperzell and Haslangkreit in the east – are privately owned now, several of them as the seats of noble families who continue to enjoy respect among the populace and play a role in their communities.

People are fiercely fond of tradition, and the female folkwear among the Aichach rural community has lasted an astonishingly long time. To this day the traditional puffed dress, spencer jacket and apron are worn not only at special events but are often seen in everyday life. At religious as well as secular events, women wearing folk dress are popular with photographers – but that is when they wear typically Bavarian clothing at its finest. Silk materials, fringed scarves and large silver buttons are all part of it. Aichach's claim to fame as an »island of folkwear« may be short-lived, however: globalization is slowly taking over, and Wittelsbacher Land is no exception.

That should be no cause for concern in the triangle between Augsburg, Munich and Ingolstadt, however. This old rural area has long been a commuter region, with a big city at its doorstep. This means career opportunities. Many have no other option but to travel between 30 and 70 kilometres to their place of work. This usually presents little difficulties, however, thanks to the well-built A8 highway from Stuttgart to Munich, the trunk roads from Augsburg to Ingolstadt and Fürstenfeldbruck and the rail links between Augsburg, Ingolstadt and Munich.

Some people who have to make the arduous daily journey to a nearby city and return home late in the evening consider their homes in Wittelsbacher Land as a sort of retreat with a unique identity that has to be carefully preserved. One good example is the small market town of Mering, which despite its good rail connection to Munich and Augsburg is anything but a soulless »dormi-

Eighteen of the former 20 towers in Friedberg's fortifications still stand today (left), and provide wonderful views across the surrounding Lech plain for those lucky enough to live inside them. Any stroll through the old town centre should include the town hall (above) and the castle with its museum – both very photogenic.

tory town« for commuters. Instead, it has retained its special character.

In Wittelsbacher Land people are not sad if the advantages of their own homeland are enjoyed by a small minority alone. The less attractive one makes oneself, the less danger there is of being monopolised. Guests can come, fine – but if they have any better ideas then they' re quite welcome to stay away too. No one is pushy in Old Bavaria. Hiking routes are marked and cycling tours suggested, but benches along the way to rest on are quite a rarity. Connoisseurs know how to arrange their healthy hikes through field and forest in such a way that they arrive at a comfortable country inn or shady beer garden at just the right point, or take along a picnic for their summer walks to the small artificial lakes between Sand and barrage 23 along the river Lech. Wherever there are sights to be seen, there are usually inns or restaurants too.

The Baroque pilgrimage churches of Maria Birnbaum in Ecknachtal near Sielenbach, Herrgottsruh in Friedberg and St. Leonhard in Inchenhofen are sight like these, draped in wondrous legends and full of magnificent works of art by some of Germany's greatest architects and painters. Maria Birnbaum, which once belonged to Blumenthal, is linked with master builders Konstantin Bader (Munich) and Gabriel Schwarz (Augsburg) and stucco worker Matthias Schmuzer from Wessobrunn; Herrgottsruh is famous for its frescoes by Cosmas Damian Asam; and St. Leonhard in Inchenhofen was largely decorated by Ignaz Baldauf, a court painter of the prince-bishops of Augsburg.

St. Leonhard (known locally as Leahad) has long made the small market town of Inchenhofen a very attractive place. From the 13th to the 19th centuries this pilgrimage to the patron saint of prisoners, pregnant women, farmers and cattle was one of the most important in Europe.

Today thousands of visitors still flock to the town for its Leonhardiritt festival on the first Sunday in November and admire the magnificently decorated carnival floats. People in costume act out scenes from the life of St. Leonhard; this requires great stamina in case of frost or rain, because the actors are not allowed to move. During the entire trip through the town, they remain fixed in position like wax figures.

Another public attraction in a far-flung corner of Wittelsbacher Land has also braved quite a few tests of strength: the Hofberg Theatre in Schiltberg. Every two years the permanent stage, designed to look like a medieval castle, is the scene of historical open-air performances. The local amateur actors, on horseback and armed with swords, have had numerous successes since the tradition began in 1953.

The Friedberger Zeit festival, in the old town of Friedberg, is a rather more modern tradition. This town, with its thick walls and towers that were once used as a bulwark by Bavaria in an attempt to fend off mighty Augsburg, has attracted visitors to its festival since 1989. Tolls are no longer charged these days, but a large deposit has to be paid for the use of the large clay beermugs jointly raised in celebration by the Friedbergers and their former Augsburg enemies.

One unusual event in Aichach has now become well-known beyond the region: the annual meeting of the »Royal Bavarian Party of St. Joseph.« Its members want to have St. Joseph's Day (March

The Knights of the Teutonic Order in Blumenthal commissioned the pilgrimage church of Maria Birnbaum near Sielenbach (right). The awe-inspiring town gates of Aichach (above), leading to its historic centre with the town hall and the Spitalkirche. Kühbach Castle (below) once formed part of a Benedictine convent.

19th) reintroduced as a public holiday, and anyone who wants to join has to adopt the name Joseph, regardless of whether they were christened Otto, Alfred or Eduard.

There are many more reasons to visit Wittelsbacher Land. Some people like to stroll through the old ducal towns of Friedberg and Aichach, or through the market towns and villages between Pöttmes and Steindorf. Others like looking for bargains at the numerous flea markets and fairs. During asparagus season Wittelsbacher Land gets a large number of visitors, all of whom came to Schrobenhausen in younger years to buy their asparagus because it was cheaper and fresher there than in Augsburg. The farmers of Aichach-Friedberg are almost Swabian in the way they do business deals with the Augsburgers at this time of the year, and the famed Schrobenhausen asparagus is now being grown very close to the Lech plain itself. The farmer's market beside the highway in Dasing is just as much of a magnet to visitors as the water-diviners and faith healers of the region, whose addresses are considered insider tips. Any visitors who find the rather gruff people here rather difficult to deal with sometimes should never make the mistake of underestimating them.

Above left: Since 2000, from July to November, the Sisi Castle in Unterwittelsbach near Aichach (above) has hosted several exhibitions on the legendary Austrian empress Elisabeth (Sisi). This idyllically situated, moated castle was the favourite summer residence of Sisi's father, Duke Max of Bavaria, from 1838 to 1850.
Below left: The Neo-Gothic altar in the Church of St. Peter and Paul in Pöttmes, which was built in 1478.

No, Wittelsbacher Land never had an Asterix or an Obelix. But it did have the robber and poacher Matthäus Klostermair, who became famous in 18th-century Swabia as the Bayrischer Hiasl. The son of a day labourer from Kissing, he robbed the establishment whenever he could and, much like Robin Hood, distributed his booty among the poor – until he was captured in Osterzell, near Kaufbeuren, and executed very nastily in Dillingen in 1771.

Good examples of the sensible private and public use of historic buildings: Scherneck Castle (above), near Rehling, and the former monastery of Thierhaupten (below) in the district of Augsburg. After thorough renovation the monastery is now used as a centre for improvement of villages and the countryside.

During the 19th century, pretty waitress Coletta Möritz from Ebenried near Pöttmes became popular in a very different way. The Munich painter Friedrich August Kaulbach »discovered« the attractive »beer girl« from The Sternecker Brewery in the valley as a model for his famous Schützenlisl motif. He painted her as a happy waitress dancing on a beer-barrel with 10 litre-size glasses of beer in her hands. At the seventh Munich archery contest held in 1881, the 5-metre-high painting hung above the entrance to a beer tent and caused a furore. It was later immortalised on thousands of postcards.

One kindred spirit of the Old Bavarians in Swabia was the writer Ludwig Thoma, who used to go hunting in the Aichach hinterland. Many of his tales, socially critical plays and novels take place in a rural milieu. The same area has produced two marvellously satirical cabaret groups: the folk group known as Biermösl Blosn and its gifted female counterpart, the Wellküren. – Which brings us back to the local government reorganisation and its rather wilful redistribution of borders: the so-called »Aichach Hinterland«, where Ludwig Thoma used to go hunting and the Biermösl Blosn have their home, has since 1972 actually belonged to the market town of Altomünster and thus no longer to Aichach at all but to the district of Dachau in Upper Bavaria. And several people are still annoyed about that. *Manuela Mayr*

Competition is good for business – it's a truism that applies in many areas of life. When towns compete with each other, the result is similar: he townspeople usually profit from the ambition o do better than one's neighbour. Memmingen versus Kempten. In this day nd age, one shouldn't imagine a person from Memmingen suddenly being eized by anger whenever ne meets anyone from Kempten, or the towns' wo mayors only grudgingly shaking hands with each other. That would be oo much. But if one town nanages to lure a major ndustrial enterprise into heir town – and hence a otential taxpayer with a arge number of new jobs – hen hands do tend to get ubbed together in glee at the neighbouring town osing out.

Even though Memmingen is unable to style itself the »metropolis of the Allgäu«, and with its 41,000 or so nhabitants is »only« the third-largest town behind Kempten and Kaufbeuren, this former free imperial city (it was elevated to municipal status in 1191) still plays a dominant role in the Allgäu.

Economy: The motorway junction with connections o Munich, Lake Constance and Ulm gives the town a ecure central location that is one of the main reasons why major firms are so attracted to it. The industrial reas around it are expanding all the time, and busiess is booming. The town has been a leading business centre since 1993.

A look back to the year 1957: it was announced that et planes would be transferred to the air-base at Memmingerberg instead of the planned helicopter school. People were worried at first, and there were protests rom the local and regional councils – mainly because of the noise pollution that would result. All to no avail, however. On May 5, 1959 the then defence

Memmingen and the Lower Allgäu

minister Franz-Josef Strauss travelled in person to the Lower Allgäu and officially brought Fighter-Bomber Squadron 34 into service. The local politicians soon changed their minds about the noise pollution when they realized that the squadron was bringing their region economic prosperity and new jobs. This explains all the noisy protests last year when defence minister Rudolf Scharping announced that the squadron would be forced to leave Memmingerberg. Memmingen's mayor Holzinger complained that the loss of so many jobs would mean serious economic difficulties for Memmingen and the surrounding area. The decision seemed irreversible, however, which is why people are now wondering how to use the airfield in future. There are two conflicting schools of thought: one camp wants a civil airport, and has provided suitable plans for it, while the other is against any more aeroplanes and keeps on reminding everyone of the terrible noise pollution of the past years.

Memmingen has always been able to profit from its strategic location as far as traffic is concerned. It must have been keen political wits and a good feel for trade that brought Memmingen a lead role in Germany at a time when the guilds were taking over from noble families. A self-confident populace emerged early on, and Humanism and the arts flourished – the Strigel family of artists, for instance, gained great recognition. Trading routes led as far as India and Venezuela. In around 1530 the townspeople adopted the Lutheran faith. They had to suffer much, because the Thirty Years' War left its traces too – the town had to endure three sieges, several months of occupation by Wallenstein as well as by King Gustav Adolf of Sweden, and also plagues, deaths and famine. A period of political decline set in from 1648, and lasted until the 19th century. Then there was a change from centuries of democratic self-rule to the authorities of a principality, and in 1803 Memmingen became a part of Bavaria.

Culture: Cultural life in Memmingen is not only many-faceted but very often first-class. One reason for this is the large number of halls and centres in the town. Take the Stadthalle, or main concert hall, for instance, which is one of the largest and most modern of its kind in the region. Stars and starlets from the world of pop and rock music are regular performers here, regularly attracting a large public from all over the area. Wolfgang Ambros, Gerhard Polt, Konstantin Wecker, and jazz greats such as Joe Zawinul or Pat Metheny, Haindling or Richie Blackmore have all performed recently on the stage of the Stadthalle. If the 1000 seats in the hall are not enough, the concert organizers switch the event to the nearby Eissporthalle (Ice Hockey Hall), which was completed in 1987 and can hold up to 5,500 people. The highlights here have been concerts by Joe Cocker, Peter Maffay, Herbert Grönemeyer, Bryan Adams or Modern Talking.

The Stadttheater (Town Theatre), with its 450 seats, is an altogether more dignified place. Up until the Reformation, this building in the middle of the pedestrian precinct served as a monastery tithe barn; it was converted into the municipal armoury in 1620, and finally turned into a theatre in 1802. Conversion work took place on it in 1905 and again in 1974, when the foyer was added. The year 1953 is an important one in Memmingen cultural history: that was when the Swabian Local Theatre Association was founded. It formed the economical basis for the town's own professional theatre ensemble. Six performances in the Stadttheater and just as many in the town's smaller Theater am Schweizerberg form the subscription series in Memmingen. The »Theatre and Culture Association« also provides a classical concert series. Walter Weyers, the man in charge of it at present, made a name for himself nationwide with the world premiere of Clytemnestra, a rock opera with music by David Defeis. It was the first part of a trilogy, in fact, which continued with The Rebels in 2001 and ended in June 2003 with Lilith.

The Antonierhaus is a cultural gem. According to an old certificate, King Friedrich II (1212–1250) presented the hospital of St. Anthony in the episcopal diocese of Vienne, a patron of the Antonites, with the right of patronage of his church of St. Martin in Memmingen with all the accompanying rights. Although it is unlikely that Memmingen is the oldest centre of the Antonites in Germany, the hospital of St. Anthony soon won the town international significance. Memmingen's located at the intersection of two important trading routes combined with the hospital's reputation to make the town economically successful. The Antonite base farthest to the southeast was also entrusted with the bishoprics of the ecclesiastical province of Salzburg, the dioceses of Augsburg, Chur or Trent. Today the former hospital contains a municipal library as well as the Strigel and Antonite Museums.

Traditions: The Fischertag, or Fishermen's Day in July each year is a high festival for this town. Centuries old, the custom dates back to the former tradition of cleaning the small river through Memmingen and is a must in the social calendar, especially for the members of the town's fishing club – although numerous Memmingers return to their native town for the event too. The decoratively dressed children begin the festivities on the Thursday. Thousands of them listen to the speech given at 10am from the balcony in the Market Square by the mayor. The moment when the thousands of children all start to sing their songs in the flag-adorned market square is very moving. The next day half the town is on its feet, after the messenger with the bells has announced that »fishing has begun« and left the Town Hall at 6pm, and after the first cannonade has been fired by the town guard. Many

Page 74, inset: A hidden view of the church tower of St. Martin.
Page 75: The heart of Memmingen, the Market Square with the Fountain and Town Hall.
Right: The Stadtbach, or »town stream«.
Below: The Market Place with the Fountain and the Town Hall.

Above: The market place in Memmingen with the fountain, the Steuerhaus (right) and St. Martin in the background.
Left: The Mindelburg Fortress near Mindelheim.

pubs and restaurants attract visitors with open-air meals, and a great deal of alcohol is consumed. The night is brief, of course: at 7am on the Saturday, all the fishermen (men only!), surrounded by shouting and cheering crowds, are ordered to jump into the river and hunt down the biggest trout. Later the new Fisher King is placed on his royal throne in the stadium hall. The festival has been going for quite some time, despite some recent disapproval about cruelty to animals and complaints about it being an outmoded bastion of male chauvinism. That criticism has not been enough to stop the long tradition, however.

The second major event in Memmingen's year is the Wallenstein Spiele, or Wallenstein Games. It was in May 1630 that Albrecht Wenzel Eusebius Wallenstein, Duke of Friedland, Mecklenburg and Sagan, marched through Swabian territory – with his court and retinue in tow, naturally enough. He marched into Memmingen on May 30, and things were not much fun for the population from then on. Apparently Wallenstein's first order was that all the dogs and chickens in the town should be locked away, and the church bells silenced. This is apparently because the duke was not only plagued by gout but also highly sensitive to noise. Wallenstein and his retinue stayed in the town until October 3, by which time they had not only caused the people of Memmingen numerous problems but had also, and most fortunately, left money in the town. After all, the horses and riders had to be cared for – in return for cash. The local traders and craftsmen also managed to sell several items. In 1978, the Fischertag association decided to make Wallenstein the theme of a performance at the 1980 Fishing Festival. Hermann Pfeifer, a gifted songwriter and poet, sat down at his desk and started making copious notes. The result was a historical popular play about the events of the year 1530. It was followed by a parade and celebrations, and eventually by the decision to commemorate Wallenstein's march into Memmingen on a regular basis.

Left page: The Carthusian monastery in Buxheim, with the monastery church of St. Maria. The choir stalls are among the most-prized cultural relics in South Germany.
Right: A magnificent sundial at the Carthusian monastery in Buxheim.

This developed into the Wallenstein Games, during which the burghers re-enact the events of the past, sell products from that time, and sometimes even live the way people used to 350 years ago.

Sport: In 1987, the town was swept by hockey fever when the decision was made to build a new ice hockey stadium on the Hühnerberg. At the end of November it was inaugurated with a game between the SCM and Bad Reichenhall, and the place was sold out. An audience of 3,200 spectators is a record for any club in the regional league. The enthusiasm continued unabated, and the club's fortunes improved with every week that passed. The first team gradually made it into the second-highest category in Germany. Professional ice hockey in a small town – and suddenly the SCM started producing national-level players. The average attendance for any game was 3,000. Since that time, the SCM has experienced economic problems, and its follow-up club (EHC) has been playing in the senior league.

Football fans in Memmingen can also remember great days. In the stadium of the Bodenseestrasse, the FCM was always a member of the highest amateur league, and always earned a fortune whenever its rivals FC Augsburg or 1860 Munich were guests. The viewing record was in 1986 when over 8,000 spectators turned up to watch a game against the »Lions« from Munich. Today Memmingen football club is in the national league.

Sights: Memmingen sights include the churches, such as the Frauenkirche. First mentioned in 1258, it was decorated in the Gothic era, probably by Hans Strigel. There is also the Church of St. Martin: its walls are also decorated with valuable works by Hans and Bernhard Strigel. It also has impressive Gothic choir stalls.

Another good church is the Kreuzherrnkirche: originally Gothic, it has one of the most valuable ceilings in South Germany with stucco work by the famous Wessobrunn School. Houses worth visiting include the Siebendächerhaus or »Seven-Roofed House«, once used by tanners for pelts; the Grimmelhaus, which today contains the municipal culture centre, the culture office and also the adult education centre, the Parishaus, built in the year 1736; the Town Hall, built in 1589; and the Steuerhaus, built in 1495 and given an additional storey in 1708. The latter once housed the tax authorities, but today is simply an administrative building.

Buxheim. This quiet little spa town possesses a real cultural gem: one of the best-preserved Carthusian monasteries in Germany. It underwent conversion work in the 15th and 18th centuries. The richly-carved choir stalls of the Gothic monastery church, with its cloister and baroque interior decoration, are an absolute masterpiece; much money and hard work have been invested in this historical site over the past years.

Schloss Lautrach: Once a meeting place for artists and scientists, this former princes' residence dating from the 18th century is today a much-visited conference centre for managers from all over Germany. The Management Centre here also has an exclusive four-star hotel attached to it. The décor is most impressive, as are the grounds surrounding the establishment.

Kronburg: The castle is impossible to miss, in its dominant position high above the River Iller. It dates from the Renaissance, and anyone taking a closer look inside its walls will realise that much of historical interest is here to be visited. Baron and Baroness von Vequel-Westernach are happy to take visitors on personal tours of this impressive castle. Schloss Kronburg today is the perfect venue for classical music concerts, castle courtyard festivals or elaborate banquets.

Right: The Basilica of Ottobeuren is utterly majestic.
Below: The inner courtyard of the Renaissance castle of Kronburg.

Left, and facing page: The pilgrimage church of Maria Steinbach, a gem of South German church architecture.

Maria Steinbach: This small community attracts pilgrims once each year – their destination is the rococo church of Maria Steinbach, a gem of South German church architecture containing an organ built by the famous Joseph Gabler. In 1986 there was an unfortunate accident here when part of the ceiling's stucco decoration fell off during Whitsun. Since that time the equivalent of 2.3 million Euros have been spent on renovation work, and today the church has been restored to its former glory.

Ottobeuren: This spa town in the grassy valley of the Günz attracts an international clientele each year to its Benedictine abbey, founded in 764, which in the 18th century was extended to form the largest monastery complex in all of South Germany. The masterpiece here is the basilica, built between 1737 and 1766. Simpert Kramer drew up the original plans for this colossal structure, which was finally completed by Johann Michael Fischer. Every year, masterpieces by the greatest composers are performed in the basilica, which has room for an audience of 2,500. The ensembles are always first-class, as are the conductors. The visitors' book at Ottobeuren contains such great names as Herbert von Karajan, Leonard Bernstein, Wolfgang Sawallisch, Eugen Jochum and Günter Wand. Culture is very much alive and well in Ottobeuren – the town even has a famous painter living in it, Diether Kunerth, and there are plans to devote a museum exclusively to his work.

Mindelheim: Mindelheim became Bavarian in 1801, and was given a magistrates' constitution 17 years later. This town, with its 14,000 inhabitants, not only has a historic old section but also the Mindelburg fortress, where the peasant leader Georg von Frundsberg once resided. The big folk festival in this town is the Frundsbergfest. Sights worth seeing here include the Rathauseck, the gates, towers and alleyways of the old town, the Jesuit Chapel and the Liebfrauen Chapel, and four museums.

Freddy Schissler

The Eastern Allgäu

The Eastern Allgäu is definitely a jewel, and most especially its southern region, which is a sapphire when one considers the sheer wealth of lakes here. One of the most majestic of them is the Alpsee, near Hohenschwangau. King Ludwig II, who swam across it in just under 20 minutes, wanted to span the lake at one stage with a romantic cableway in the form of a peacock-shaped gondola. The King was also delighted by Lohengrin singer Paul von Thurn & Taxis, who crossed the lake in a small open boat while singing the swan-knight's arias to the accompaniment of the Kempten infantry regiment band (the latter, to keep things suitably Wagnerian, had to hide behind some bushes). Summer evenings here are a perfect opportunity to »wallow in kitsch« here, when the archaic-sounding Schwangau alphorns boom out across the lake from the Pindarplatz. If you swim in the Alpsee, you will see both royal castles: the saffron-yellow Hohenschwangau and the deathly-pale Neuschwanstein. Surprisingly, just a few steps away from the mass tourism around these castles, there is an enchanted world of silence and mythological solitude. Take the sleepy Schwanensee Park, for instance, the Wittelsbach family's smaller version of Munich's Englischer Garten, with its 5,000 species of tree. Or the highly atmospheric Gnomensteig, a path leading from the furthest corner of the Alpsee up to the Marienbuche, through a natural amphitheatre of mighty limestone cliffs. Continue from the Alpsee to the no less mysterious Alatsee, in the Faulenbach Valley near Füssen. It has the second-highest concentration of hydrogen sulphide of any lake in central Europe, which is why

Facing page: Neuschwanstein Castle towering above the mist covering the Alpsee, with the Tannheimer and Vilser Mountains in the background. Photo: Getty Images/Merten.
Above left: The Neuschwanstein Musical Theatre on the shore of the Forggensee near Füssen.
Below left: Hohenschwangau Castle, located between the majestic Alpsee and the small and sleepy Schwansee.

divers at depth of five metres or more can no longer see their hands in front of their faces. The ancient paths along the Alatsee are similarly hard to make out: smugglers used them to take cheese and livestock to nearby Tyrol, and to bring back tobacco and coffee. Was the gold of the Deutsche Reichsbank really dumped in the Alatsee just before the end of World War II? No one knows for certain. Miniature submarines were once tested here, however – as evinced by the still-visible concrete ramp on the lake's eastern shore. Below the Alatsee is the fish-rich Weissensee, with possibly the finest presbytery in the whole of the Allgäu. The building, with its square groundplan, is overgrown with reeds and has a special entrance reserved for the pastoral rowing-boat. Above the Weissensee, hidden in the mountain forest, is the Magnussitz, a rocky outcrop where the Allgäu apostle St. Magnus is supposed to have rested after having noisily ploughed the Magnus Alp higher up, and also taught the Alemannians here the basics of agriculture, mining and smelting of iron ore. The Magnus Mine at the Älpeleskopf below the Säuling still exists today, as does the oratory that the Rhaeto-Romanic apostle from the monastery of St. Gallen founded beside the River Lech in the middle of the 8th century AD. It developed into the magnificent Benedictine monastery of Sankt Mang. The saint's mortal remains have been lost without trace, but his footprint on the Lusalten, where he took an enormous running jump across the thundering Lech Waterfall to escape the demons chasing him, has been preserved to this day; the place is both an Early Christian cult site and a tourist attraction. Luckily, not many people know that only a few metres below the Magnus Footprint, located rather daringly 30 metres above the foaming river Lech (which forces its way here through a terminal moraine and into the foothills of the Alps), there is a »bolt-hole«, probably Celtic in origin, to symbolically remove all the evil. À propos jumping: in the Schwangau one can »jump geologically« straight into the mountains. The wild and romantic Pöllat Gorge begins at the foot of the Neuschwanstein castle rock. A hike through this gorge and then up to the famous castle itself is a walk through millions of years of geological history, and is also exactly the same route taken by the peasants and firemen of the Schwangau when they wanted to prevent King Ludwig II from being arrested. Today the monarch, with his »Yearning for Paradise«, sinks beneath the waters of an artificial Lake Starnberg around 400 times a year – on Germany's largest rotating stage at the Neuschwanstein Musical Theatre near Füssen. The Forggensee, formed by the dammed-up Lech, is the fifth-largest lake in Bavaria. Forty years ago the villages of Forggen and Deutenhausen sank beneath its waters, together with the Illasberg ra-

Above, from left to right: The former Benedictine monastery of St. Mang towers above the Füssener Lechhalde. The inner courtyard of the Hohes Schloss in Füssen, with its trompe-l'oeil wall frescoes. View from the Hohes Schloss across the roof of Füssen's Franciscan monastery as far as the Tegelberg, the Schwangau's »local mountain«.
Facing page: Hohenschwangau Castle and the Prinzenbau tower above the boathouse on the picturesque Alpsee.

vine and part of the old Roman Via Claudia Augusta. Not far away from the Tiefes Tal, or »Deep Valley«, near Rosshaupten, where Magnus the missionary is supposed to have killed a dragon, the Via Claudia Art Park combines the modern and the traditional, and makes a good stopping-place just beside the Strada del Sole. Nearby, surrounded by rolling moraine landscape, stands the birthplace of the famous lute-maker Caspar Tieffenbrucker who, according to recent research, may even have invented the violin. Tieffenbrucker was probably one of the Eastern Allgäu's first mächeler (a person who likes doing fiddly or finicky things), a tradition leading to Erwin Wöhrler from Weissensee who in 1963 invented the cow-tail-holder for the traditional cattle stable, as well as to the boffins in the Innova High Tech Park in Kaufbeuren who make high-speed cameras for NASA.

Just to take one example among many, if one looks at the gentle forests, meadows and moors of the landscape directly beneath the 1,054-metre-high Auerberg, also known as the »Swabian Rigi«, the Eastern Allgäu is transformed from a sapphire into an emerald. The natural colours here are like a musical composition: from the Ada-

Right: Taking a break at the Forggensee near Füssen, with the »mad king's castle« in the background, framed by the Tegelberg, Bleckenau and Säuling.
Below, left to right: The baroque pilgrimage church of St. Coloman, located in the middle of the countryside near Schwangau. A rural idyll near Füssen. The pilgrimage church of Maria-Hilf in Speiden. Pebble beaches on the so-called »Banana Islands« in the Forggensee. The 1800-metre-high Tegelberg near Schwangau is a paradise for paragliding and hang-gliding.

gio of the earth tones in the moorland and the Andante of dark-green fir trees to the Allegro of light-green beech leaves and the Capriccio of juicy-green May meadows filled with bright-yellow dandelions. To stay with greenery briefly, the formerly Roman Via Claudia Augusta, now a popular cycling path, has had an old species of cider-pear planted on it, while the jewel of nature known as the Birnbaumer Filz near Trauchgau contains several American oak-trees – a quirk of post-war history. Far older, in the hamlet named Sameister, is the chapel consecrated to the Seven Pains of Mary, an artistic jewel with its striking windows and the tomb of »Eastern Allgäu Palladio« Johann Jakob Herkomer. The myriad emerald hues of the landscape can be equally well appreciated from the 1,268-metre-high Falkenstein near Pfronten, Germany's highest ruined castle; and the same applies to the so-called »Acropolis of the Allgäu«, the two ruined medieval castles of Hohenfreyberg and Eisenberg. Legend has it that their two eye-catching mounds were left behind as clods of clay from the boots of a giant.

Nature, history, art and culture, all of it set in the midst of a very fortunate landscape and framed against the heroic mountain backdrop of the Königswinkel – it is all highly characteristic of the Eastern Allgäu, and soon the emerald changes to a ruby with just as many facets. These range from the Passion Playhouse of the market town of Waal in the north of the region to the King Ludwig Musical in the south. From

the former Free Imperial City of Kaufbeuren with its Tänzelfest, Bavaria's oldest children's festival, and Bavaria's youngest saint Crescentia, to the city of Füssen on the Lech. This is where the first lutemaker's guild in Europe was formed in the mid-15th century, and the »Peace of Füssen« ended the Bavarian-Austrian War of Secession. The Emperor Maximilian I, the Last Knight, stayed in Füssen's Late Gothic »High Castle« on at least 40 occasions, complete with his famous court orchestra. The memento mori is an iconographic leitmotif in Füssen's monastery of Sankt Mang, culminating in the Dance of Death in the Anna Chapel, painted by Jakob Hiebeler. Indeed, music still links the whole of the Eastern Allgäu today, from the Füssen Ancient Music Festival and the European Organ Competition to the castle concerts at Neuschwanstein and the Bavarian Music Academy in the regional Allgäu town of Marktoberdorf. The Academy has now moved to the former summer residence of Augsburg elector Clemens Wenzeslaus on the Schlossberg, from where it organises the world-famous Musica Sacra festival as well as the no less prestigious International Chamber Choir Competition. The Bavarian Regional Youth Jazz Orchestra is based in the inn at the castle, and the former gatehouse has been revived as a creative »composing house« in the summertime for young musical talent. The East Allgäu Bürgermeister Chorus, in contrast, is active all year round, and there are also more brass bands to be found here than anywhere else in Germany. There are further musical curiosities in the district of Schwangau, two being the »Kaiser Wilhelm Memorial Band« and the »Erlisholz Mountain Drum Preservation Society«. To the regret of many, they both limit their performances to the Carnival season. In view of the vast amount of culture on offer, this list is necessarily incomplete, but the »Klang & Raum« Festival is definitely worth a special mention. In the baroque splendour of the former Benedictine abbey of Irsee, Bruno Weil and his Canadian orchestra »Tafelmusik« bring the Vienna Classical epoch back to life. The abbey has something of a dark history, however: during the Nazi era, the nursing home in Irsee was the main euthanasia centre in Bavaria. The modern, forward-looking village of Irsee has now overcome such past blemishes, however, and has won several state-wide »golden village« prizes, one of them for its 4-star hotel for horses.

The colourful gems of the Eastern Allgäu are certainly an integral part of Bavarian Swabia's splendour. On one of those endlessly sunny, blue-skied days, sit on the wooden terrace at the Beichelstein Alp near Seeg, enjoy some delicious local mountain cheese or some home-made cake, and take in the view from the Ammer Mountains and the nearby »Tannheim Dolomites« all the way to the Aggenstein and the Edelsberg. At such times it's hard not to feel grateful that you actually live in a landscape where everyone else comes for their holidays!

Andrea Zinnecker

Facing page: The market town of Nesselwang with its parish church of St. Andreas, against the backdrop of the Ammergau Alps.
Below, left to right: Taking a stroll along a lime-tree avenue in Marktoberdorf.
Church towers and rooftops in the old part of Kaufbeuren.
Part of the medieval town wall.
The Fünfknopfturm tower, still inhabited today, is the symbol of Kaufbeuren.

HOTEL

The Residenz in Kempten was the sacred and secular centre of Kempten Abbey until secularisation. The baroque building contains largely original state rooms such as the Throne Room, the largest of the chambers inside.

Kempten

The valleys are still filled with fog. At the Waltenberger Haus, high up in the mountains of Oberstdorf, Mandi Böllmann is serving her guests breakfast at her mountain hut. Down in the villages, the farmers are driving their cattle to pasture. Thousands of people are travelling to work. At Bosch in Blaichach, the night shift is just ending. The guests at the spa of Oberstaufen are starting the day in cold, wet sheets. In the »Alpine Allergy Station Oberjoch« the patients are taking a good deep breath of first-class fresh air. A noticeably large number of tractors and cattle transporters are annoying motorists today in the »Allgäu metropolis« of Kempten. A large auction is being held in the animal breeding hall. Just a few metres away, the new and ultra-modern »Forum Allgäu« shopping centre is just opening, with its 23,000 square metres of floor space and massive, multi-purpose hall ...

The Upper Allgäu has many faces, but a single unique profile – moulded by the landscape as well as the special people who live there. To get an overall idea of Swabia's southernmost region, why not do what the locals love doing repeatedly: climb a mountain? The 1,738-metre-high Grünten, also known as the »Guardian of the Allgäu« because of its exposed location, provides a breathtaking panoramic view of one of Germany's most attractive landscapes.

and the Upper Allgäu

The Hofgarten, once the baroque garden of the Residenz, is bordered decoratively to the north by the Orangery, which today houses the town library.

View from the Hofgarten to the Basilica of St. Lorenz in Kempten, the first large church to be built in South Germany after the Thirty Years' War. The interior of the structure features a fine combination of Late Renaissance and Early Baroque elements.

In the south is the striking-looking Allgäuer Hauptkamm, the main ridge, with its peaks that remain snow-covered well into summer. »An exemplary collection of every conceivable Alpine formation« is how it was described by the Swabian naturalist Dr. Alfred Weitnauer (1905–74). The mountain range is around 10 million years old, and the peaks are as high as 2,600 metres. Nowhere else in the Alps are the mountains as differently shaped as they are here: the Gottesacker Plateau, with its desolate areas of karst, the far gentler-looking Nagelfluhkette, the pointed peaks of the Siplinger Köpfe, and the rocky wilderness of the Trettach and the Mädelegabel. And right at the centre, Höfats and Schneck, with grass and flowers still growing as high as 2,000 metres on the rough slopes of their summits. The hundreds of peaks, ridges and gorges here leave an unforgettable impression, and are a popular area for climbers, skiers and mountain-bikers.

Gaze from the peak of the Grünten to the north now. The view is full of meadows, forests, lakes, rivers, villages and towns. The appearance of the Upper Allgäu today was largely created by the glaciers that carved their way into the valley 20,000 years ago, leaving a moraine landscape full of countless small hills, lakes and high moorland behind – but farmers have also made their mark on this landscape. Indeed, this Alpine cultural landscape was only formed by their hard labour: as far back as the Middle Ages they cut trees up to the 1,000-metre level to gain room for agriculture. These days it is almost impossible to imagine how difficult it must have been to farm these steep slopes – two hundred years ago, the Upper Allgäu was still one of Germany's most impoverished regions. It was Carl Hirnbein who changed the situation in 1830, when he ended the relatively unsuccessful farming activity in the region and introduced the art of cheesemaking – which made all the slopes as green as they are today.

Today it is impossible to imagine the hills of the Allgäu without the typical brown cows grazing on them – or the covers of glossy tourist brochures, for that matter. When Alfred Weitnauer referred to the cow as »the uncrowned queen of the Allgäu« in 1958, it was almost prophetic, because to minimise injuries in stables, many cows in the region are indeed »uncrowned« – their horns are removed early on. Thanks to digital retouching of bro-

chure photographs, however, this small problem can easily be concealed.

Everyone knows the photos of the traditional Allgäu cattle herds. During the traditional Almabtrieb, thousands of cows are driven back down into the valleys from the high mountain pastures. For many city dwellers in this high-tech age it is almost inconceivable that men and women spend around 100 days a year in primitively built mountain huts, with no electricity or running water. Not one of the 617 alpine pastures in the Allgäu has been closed in past years, even though dairy farming has long stopped being self-financing. Preservation of alpine culture has now adopted a primary role, and Bavarian and EU funds are keeping it going in the background. There are 96,000 cattle in the Upper Allgäu today – around two for every three people.

The cows' milk – the »white gold« of the Allgäu – is processed at numerous famous-name dairies in the region. The best known of these are the Champignon dairy, the Edelweiss Milchwerke, the Stegmann Emmentaler Käsereien and Töpfer GmbH. More cheese is produced here than anywhere else in Germany. The South German butter and cheese exchange in Kempten is today one of the most important business centres for milk products in Germany. Cheese is not the only successful export, however. According to a study by Kempten University, only 20 percent of people immediately associate the Allgäu with cheese; other successful local products include rolling and milling machines made by Liebherr, ABS braking systems by Bosch in Blaichach, and stockings by the firm of Kunert in Immenstadt.

»Work where others go on holiday!« is a common advertisement by local firms. A great deal of people come to South Germany's southernmost region for their holidays. The handful of visitors who came here seeking mountain spas 130 years ago have today been replaced by 2.5 million guests annually. Tourism is the most important economic motor of the region, with 11 million registered overnight stays each year. The most popular tourist destination is Oberstdorf, the region's oldest and most celebrated mountain spa. Locals are definitely in the minority here: according to the statistics, there are 1.7 guest beds in town for each Oberstdorfer. Even international stars such as Tina Turner think very highly of holidays in the spa centre of Oberstaufen, and no less a person than the Aga Khan is a great fan of Bad Hindelang, a much-acclaimed ecological centre. »Farmhouse Holidays« are an important source of income to the local farmers, and an attractively cheap alternative to a hotel for families. In the southern part of the region, one in two farmers provides holiday apartments.

What is it that attracts people here every year, despite the availability of guaranteed sunshine and snow at cheap charter destinations the world over? The weather in the Allgäu is notoriously unpredictable, after all, and even though the amount of sunshine here is almost as high as in Germany's sunniest town, Freiburg, some holidays can be completely rained off. Perhaps it is the nostalgic yearning for intact nature, and the natural and uncomplicated view of life shared by those who live here.

The landscape around Sonthofen is especially attractive.
Left: The spa resort of Bühl on the Grosser Alpensee near Immenstadt, one of the largest natural lakes in the Allgäu.

Rather than bend over backwards to help and promote tourism, the people of the Upper Allgäu remain true to themselves. Even special spa and wellness attractions have a local flavour: guests at several hotels have the option of bathing in whey, or rolling in hay. One hotel in Bad Hindelang insists that all its German guests use the familiar »Du« form of address from the very start, and has a special »hay playroom« for children. This is the distinctive feature of Allgäu tourism. Perhaps that is why the guests keep on returning to this corner of Swabia – because of the gentle charm of the landscape and its people. »Forward-looking tradition« is one of the tourism slogans of this area. The traditional and the modern, the urban and the rural, and the silent and the noisy are closer together here than in many other regions – one visit to Kempten's annual consumer exhibition makes that very clear. Milking machines, fashions, hay-drying devices, high-tech appliances, forklift trucks and a culture and entertainment programme with over 300 events all contribute to it. There is also a »milk tent« that is probably unique in all Germany, where absolutely everything is milk-related. Around 150,000 visitors a year come to the numerous tents and exhibition halls.

The biggest social event in the local calendar is Kempten's Allgäu Festival in August, however. Visiting a beer or wine tent in the evening with friends on at least one occasion is a social must, and that goes for young and old alike. The beer tents are full of oompah bands, grilled chickens and Oktoberfest-style Gemütlichkeit. The 50 or so tents for the festival have been a firm fixture in the town centre for over 50 years now, and the public is mixed to say the least, with traditional Bavarian folkwear, short T-shirts with exposed navels, leather jackets, piercings, tattoos and embroidered braces.

Kempten (pop. 62,000) is the second-largest town in Swabia and is proud of being progress-minded – but also of its great age. Anyone who enters it via Berliner Platz to the east will realize why: the words »Oldest Town in Germany« have been chiselled into a pillar there. Cologne and Trier also have a claim to that, but the earliest-ever written mention of any German town was made by the Greek geogra-

The entrance to the magnificent Breitachklamm Gorge is not far away from Tiefenbach. The water of the River Breitach crashes and seethes its way through the narrow gorge with its vertical and sometimes overhanging walls, almost 100 metres high in places. The Breitachklamm has been open all year round to the public since 1905, and is only closed when the mountain snows are thawing.

The Upper Allgäu is distinctive for piety and a strong sense of tradition. Crosses like these are a common sight along roads and paths.

pher Strabon in 18 AD when he referred to Cambodunon, »the town by the river«. It is believed to have been a centre of Celtic occupation long before the Romans arrived, though evidence of them has yet to be found. The people of Kempten are quietly confident on that score, however.

One genuine stone witness to the past is the old fortress on a hill in the middle of the town, visible for miles around – the Burghalde. The Celtic Kempteners dug themselves in here years ago to fight the Roman legionaries who crossed the Alps under the command of Augustus Tiberius. Today the open-air stage up at the fortress features performances by such German celebrities as Nena or Hubert von Goisern, or by opera companies performing Verdi's Aida and other suitable works. The open-air cinema festival shows the latest films in front of the ancient walls. Kempten's chief archaeologist, Dr. Gerhard Eber, brought the heyday of the Roman Cambodunum (which lasted 400 years) back to life in 1987, with the Cambodunum Archaeological Park to the east of the town. People can wander here through a partially reconstructed Gallo-Roman temple area, and the original ruins of the former baths are most impressive.

In 740, after Kempten had been conquered by the Alemannians, the St. Gallen monks Magnus and Theodore founded a missionary cell in the town which would eventually become the heart of a Benedictine monastery. As an imperial abbey, this was under the rule of the king or the emperor from 1200 onwards. The abbots referred to themselves as prince-abbots from 1348, and a trading town sprang up beside the monastery which would eventually become the Protestant imperial city of Kempten. Both mini-states had their own laws and their own currency, and fought each other bitterly for centuries. »The Iron Curtain was invented in Kempten«, wrote Weitnauer, the naturalist. In 1802, however, the independence of the abbey and the town came to an end: as a result of secularisation, both of them fell to the state of Bavaria, and they were forcibly united in 1818.

Anyone who walks through Kempten today will notice the former »two faces« of the town most clearly: the pat of the town that was run by the abbey has pompous-looking structures such as the Basilica of St. Lorenz with its mighty dome – the first large religious structure to be built in Germany after the Thirty Years' War – or the former residence of the prince abbots. The baroque building contains largely preserved state rooms with some magnificent rococo decoration. The fine grounds, with orangery, granary and princely stables, still reflect the wealth and magnificence of a bygone era. The former free imperial city had its own share of important structures too, however: at the centre is the Church of St. Mang, Lutheran-Protestant ever since the Reformation, and the oldest church in the town. Local residents elaborately restored many of the patricians' houses in this largely medieval part of Kempten: the renovation work began as early as 1958, before receiving state and national subsidies from 1963 onwards.

The Rathausplatz, or Town Hall Square, at the centre of today's old town, is an attractive place to relax and watch the world go by. The elegant, Late Gothic Town Hall with its two striking-looking towers that resemble oriel windows is a meeting place for young and old alike. On warm summer evenings, the place has a special dolce vita feel to it, reminding us that Italy is not that far away.

All the cafés, bars and restaurants put their tables and chairs out of doors – and at this point one suddenly remembers that one of Kempten's touristic claims to fame is that it contains as many pubs, restau-

rants and bars as a major city. Here in front of the old Town Hall, internationally famous musicians perform in the famous Kempten »Spring Jazz« festival, attracting jazz lovers from all over the world. The festival is already far more famous than its counterpart in Burghausen. The relaxed atmosphere in Kempten's centre also makes it perfect for shopping – around half a million people come here to do so every year, even from nearby Austria. The town has an added advantage in being the only large one for miles around, of course. The main shopping street in Kempten, the Fischerstrasse, was the first pedestrian precinct in all of Swabia. Today large areas of the town centre have been closed to traffic. Around 600 shops offer a broad variety of useful and beautiful items, far away from the usual hustle and bustle of the other towns nearby.

As a place to live and work, Kempten is not everyone's cup of tea – but anyone who likes a bit of city flair, prefers a clear urban overview to the anonymity of large cities and, most importantly, likes to spend their free time in nature, has come to the right place. Even though the ski-lifts in the centre have been closed down now for lack of snow, there is a wonderful landscape on Kempten's doorstep, with mountains, lakes and rivers.

Lake Constance is only a stone's throw away, too. And so it's no wonder that Kempten also has the largest number of reingeschmeckten living in it – the local word for people who have come here from other German states to live and work.

Susanne Lorenz-Munkler

This is where holiday dreams come true.
In Oberstdorf, the oldest spa town of the Allgäu.
Left: The Loretto Chapel.
Below right: The Fellhornbahn.
An attractive hiking route up to the Nebelhorn passes rushing mountain streams.

Lindau takes over presidency of the Upper House of Parliament.« – Lindau is Germany's smallest federal state, with a surface area smaller than that of Hamburg and Bremen, but in Germany's upper house of parliament Lindau often has a decisive voice among the 17 states that make it up. Unemployment in the southwest of Germany is low, and the standard of living for its 75,000 inhabitants is relatively high. Germany's southwesternmost state also came off best in the recent »Pisa« study. Next year the premier of Lindau will be taking over the presidency of the upper chamber, though he normally lives on an island in Lake Constance, very close to Baden-Württemberg, Switzerland and Austria.

Archaeologists have a very high regard for the state of Lindau because of its important Roman remains. A few years ago a head of the emperor Augustus, as high as a man, was found in a stream in Weiler, and has now been dated to between 30 BC to 14 AD. It is assumed that the excellently preserved work of art once formed part of a colossal statue made from Carrara marble that was subsequently transported to Ger-

lake constance western allgäu

many. How the sculpture ended up in the stream, however, is still subject to dispute.

Fiction and falsehood begin our journey into the Western Allgäu and to Lake Constance. The fiction is not all that fictitious at all, however, because the region of Lindau only became part of Bavaria and Swabia in 1956.

After World War II the Western Allgäu became part of the French zone of occupation, as a bridgehead between the other French-occupied regions in Württemberg, Vorarlberg and the Tyrol. From September 1945 onwards, Lindau thus occupied a rather special position legally, with its own district law courts and its own chamber of commerce and industry (which is soon due to be merged with the Augsburg and Swabia chamber of commerce).

It was only in 1956 that the Bavarian premier of that time, Wilhelm Hoegner, decided to make Lindau part of his free state. The Social Democrat wooed Lindau like a bride for quite some time, and Lindau finally relented. At the »reunification« ceremony, Hoegner said: »The district of Lindau is now a jewel among the Bavarian regions which we intend to particularly honour.«

Quite a few local residents of Lindau are wondering whether anyone in the state chancellery still remembers these words from Hoegner. The question of whether Lindau actually belongs to Bavaria at all is frequently asked in Munich, usually because of the geopolitical uncertainty involved. For the people of Munich, the Chiemsee is far closer than Lake

Pages 100/101 and left: The Wasserburg Peninsula with the parish church of St. George and the Old Castle.
Right: ripe apples. – Lake Constance is Germany's second most important fruit-growing region after the Altes Land near Hamburg.

Constance, and the A96 highway that leads to the latter from Bavaria's capital has still not been fully completed.

But the dream of Lindau becoming a federal state in its own right is over. Pacta sunt servanda, as Latin scholars say, and this brings us to the upper district of Lindau and a rather interesting falsehood. A stonemason and sculptor from Scheffau, a suburb of Scheidegg, had hewn a Roman head from stone at a sculptor conference. It was almost 2 metres high and impressively Roman-looking. He then made up the story about the archaeological find, and put the head on display for all to see.

The author of a travel guide was so delighted that he strongly recommended his readers to visit the stream where the head was found. The head has now found its way back to the artist's workshop, because it had hindered renovation work on a pub. The last word about this work of art has yet to

That reminds me of a conversation with the mayor of Harare, in Zimbabwe, Africa. The colonial past of the black continent was mentioned, and one member of our delegation began a statement with the words: »When Africa was discovered ...« – whereupon the mayor replied: »We didn't need to be discovered, we've always been here!«

Perhaps the people by the lake had always been there, because of the strategically beneficial location, the plentiful food on offer, and also the water sports.

Apparently Saints Columban, Gallus and Magnus didn't like the place that much, but they decided to stay there in the name of God anyhow. Then again, it must have been hard to preach the idea of paradise to Alemannians who felt that by living at Lake Constance, they had already arrived in it.

Above left: A territorial claim that has lasted two centuries – the Bavarian lion at the entrance to Lindau harbour.
Below left: The Mang Tower in Lindau harbour.
Above right: The symbol of the island city – the Lindavia Fountain beyond the Town Hall.
Below right: Lighthouse at the harbour mole.

be spoken, however. The falsehood continues: the creator of the sculpture has informed everyone that the head of Augustus is being renovated at the moment, and that parts of the right foot and the left hand of the statue have also been found.

Romans were supposed to have lived along the shores of Lake Constance during the first four centuries AD – but then again, the Romans were everywhere. The ones here were generally calm and unruffled in their treatment of foreigners.

The Western Allgäu has something to suit all tastes. In the lower part of the region, by the lake, the average annual temperature is between 8 and 9 degrees Celsius, and fruit and wine grow in abundance. The milk comes from the hill country around Hergensweiler, Opfenbach, Hergatz, Gestratz, Grünenbach, Maierhöfen, Weissensberg and Sigmarszell, where elevations reach 750 metres. The mountain cheese is provided by the upper part of the region, between Lindenberg, Stiefenhofen and Scheidegg.

Spring down here starts a full month earlier than in Augsburg, and the magnolia are often in bloom on Lake Constance when snow is still being shovelled along the Lech and Wertach rivers. Up north, winter lasts longer, and sudden frost in May is not unusual. Nevertheless, Bavaria's second-smallest region has three climatic zones, and its tourist potential is almost on a par with the Italian Riviera and its hinterland.

Left: Lindenberg in the Western Allgäu, with its neo-baroque parish church.
Below: Locally grown specialities – more and more districts in the Lindau region are holding weekly markets.

From skiing up in the mountains to open-air coffee at the harbour in Lindau, there is something for everyone – even the only two lighthouses in Bavaria. The tourist trade has christened this part of the world »Germany's Happy End«. It was not far from here that the first missionaries came to Bavaria, from St. Gallen and the Reichenau. Bavaria would be very different today had it not been for the Irish-Scottish monks from Lake Constance.

The region later saw numerous regents – from Bavaria, Württemberg, Austria and even France. Napoleon brought the free imperial city of Lindau to an end – something that many locals still disapprove of even today. Representatives from Munich, Vienna and Berne are not all that welcome in the area either.

The people here are aware of their own strengths. The horse traders who drove their animals as far as Italy, and the milliners who made hats from Lindau internationally famous set new standards. Today the Western Allgäu exports foodstuffs, high-tech products, chess computers, fruit juice, textiles and cooling systems to the rest of the world. The region is still favourably located: the Mediterranean begins just beyond Lake Constance, and Switzerland is a nearby trading partner that does not have to follow strict EU regulations.

The Western Allgäu also has a very special dialect, which extends as far as Vorarlberg, Appenzeller Land, Southern Baden and Alsace. The author Martin Walser, who comes from the town of Wasserburg on Lake Constance, is one of Germany's greatest contemporary writers, and has never denied his Alemannian roots. »Speaking dialect means walking barefoot through one's own language« – the old Bavarian saying has lost none of its validity. Werner Specht from Lindenberg is another person who walks barefoot: »High German is like carefully sawn planks of wood, while dialect is the fresh, growing wood of the tree itself.« The songwriter and painter is often on tour, but keeps feeling the urge to return to his home region. Even as a person from Munich, I can understand what he means.

And what about food and drink? No less a person than the brilliant French philosopher Michel de Montaigne wrote: »... there is such a huge variety of soups, sauces, and salads, and all of it prepared with such exquisite taste in the inns and restaurants here, that the cuisine of the French nobility can scarcely compare with it ...« He did write that in the 16th century, however, so the lines may need to be slightly updated.

Thomas Scherer

Left: At least the weather side of the house gets covered with shingles. Shingle-makers still exist in the region.
Below: A typical farmhouse, and a view of the picturesque landscape near Weiler.

Traditional customs are still a unique feature of the farming year, which is virtually indistinguishable from the church year. Such customs provide a sense of permanence in life, and were formerly a means of bringing different social classes together.

Trusted Traditions

The Viehscheid cattle drive in Maierhöfen. Thousands of visitors line the roadside in the first three weeks of September to watch the magnificently decorated cattle make their way down to the valley from the Alps.

There are various theories about when exactly the farming year begins. Is it during autumn sowing, or spring labour? The church year is a better guide: it begins on the first Sunday in Advent.

Both years come together on February 2 for the Feast of the Purification of the Virgin Mary, also known as Candlemas. For our forebears, it marked the end of a season filled with soot-blackened pinewood chips and tallow candles. That is why light plays a central role in the feast, and always has: daylight, and also the sort of light mentioned by old Simeon in the temple.

Both lights are symbolised by the candle and the wax stick. (As a rule, the wax stick weighs a quarter of a pound. Its so-called »wire« is six millimetres thick and three metres long.) Young farming women traditionally had to bring 25 pounds of wax sticks into their marriage, because the sticks were thought to ward off all evil. They helped against diseases, and were also brought to law courts for trials.

Every wax stick colour had its purpose too. The red ones could ward off evil by their colour, but gained much of their strength from being blessed on as many Candlemas Sundays as possible. A small nick was cut into the base of the stick for each of these

Above: Three Kings from Christertshofen. The letters C+M+B (Christus mansionem benedicat), written in chalk on the front doors of houses by the Sternsinger, are considered to be a good omen. They mean »Christ bless this house«. The Three Kings Kaspar, Melchior and Balthasar are thus welcome in every home. Below: The Leonhardiritt, or St Leonard's Ride, in Weissenhorn in the district of Neu-Ulm. St Leonhard provides assistance for all kinds of problems and ailments. Facing page: The Eselstreiben, or »Donkey Drive«, in Attenhofen – an unusual Carnival rite whereby a coachman dressed in a black frock coat drives a figure dressed entirely in straw, the so-called »donkey«. Photos: Designstudio Bauer & Partner, Neu-Ulm.

Sundays, and happiness could be passed on from one generation to the next in this way. Small sections of the stick were even hung from the right arm of household crucifixes.

The yellow wax stick was the one for grain and the pink one helped first-time mothers, while the white ones were used for funeral wreaths, the green ones helped the fruit harvest, and the blue ones meant a safe return – very useful for today's motorists.

Candlemas was also when servants were paid and exchanged. In many ways, the saying »The most impoverished homeland is better than the best job as a servant« is still relevant today.

Like Candlemas, St. Blasius Day on February 3, with its crossed candles, is also devoted to light, and the fifth of February is a special light day too: it is dedicated to St. Agatha, the patron saint of fire. Candles were also consecrated on this day in former times. In some Catholic parishes, so-called »Agatha loaves« are still baked and then blessed in church. Until the 1930s the »Agatha Blessing«, a small piece of paper bearing a blessing in Latin, was attached to the front doors of houses and stables as protection. The blessing became especially powerful if it was pressed against the head of the St. Agatha statue in the Residence Chapel in Munich. In the Cistercian convent of Oberschönenfeld it was hung from every heating niche doorway on the day in question. The long text in Latin with three crosses attached, roughly translated, meant: »Saint Agatha, give us holy beliefs and reverence for God from within. And ensure that the fatherland is freed from lava fire.«

Shrove Tuesday in Swabia has less emphasis on light, and is more varied altogether. Here, disguises are used to frighten away spirits which, though evil, are also stupid: they believe that there may be a real spirit behind the masks, so they think »better safe than sorry« and make a run for it. There are many different Swabian carnival figures, but one very common one is the Witch. She has retained her original form in Lauingen: representing winter, she strokes people's backs gently with her broom – an old fertility rite, and probably her original function.

A rather different objective is pursued by the so-called Funkenfeuer on the Sunday after Ash Wednesday. The winter, symbolised by a witch-like straw doll, is burnt, because threshed straw is popularly considered to stand for winter. Strips of burning beechwood thrown down a slope are also reminders of the rising disk of the sun.

Fasting days, which according to an old saying the Swabians would prefer to switch to fasting nights, end in Easter Week, which begins on Palm Sunday. The meaning of this day can be seen from the solemn Palm Procession. From the Ries to the Allgäu there are decorated wooden donkeys and also numerous different woven palm strips. Palm sticks with plastic eggs have never been traditional in Swabia, however.

Good Friday, with its holy graves from almost three centuries, follows Easter Night with the Easter Fire, the Easter Water and the basket of blessed food. Each family member receives an Easter pancake, a piece of ham and a red Easter egg, which is thought to represent Christ's suffering. The origin of the coloured Easter eggs is known, but according to an old custom they are laid by the Easter bunny. There are no Easter egg hunts in Swabia, however; instead the eggs lie in a »rabbit's nest«, made by children from willow rods and moss. Across the whole of Swabia the rabbit in question is summoned by phrases such as Has, Has Langoahr, leg' mir voar (»Lay me an egg, Mr. Long-Ears!«) or the rather coarser Has, has leg, oder du griagsch schläg! (»Lay rabbit, lay, or I'll clip you round the ear'ole!«)

The wood for the Swabian maypole is taken by young people from a neighbouring forest after a spirit-ridden Freinacht. It is usually a birch trunk, because there were no fir trees in Swabia before about 1870. The Bavarians' more permanent type of maypole is not generally copied by the Swabians. Whitsun is rather scanty from the festival point of view, but the waterfowl rite adds a bit of life to things: five boys have a competition, and the winner carries the decorated birch, the second the moneybag, the third a pot of grease, the fourth a basket of eggs and the fifth carries a waterfowl bound with birch or beech strips, which is then doused with water in the farmyards. This may have originated from a sacrifice to the river spirits to prevent flooding.

The Fire of St. Veit or of St. John, at the end of June, is supposed to help fertility. Whoever jumps over the flames is purified. People often ignite balls of hay and throw them into the river – possibly an old way of getting it to rain.

Above and below: The Frundsbergfest in Mindelheim takes place every three years, and is a great opportunity for dressing up and playing games. Unshaven men, wearing Renaissance costumes, pour into the town. The medieval festival, with its parades, historical games, and music and dance events commemorates the famous peasant leader Georg von Frundsberg (1473–1528). Photos: Frundsberg-Festring.

The bundle of herbs known as the Kräuterboschen during the Assumption of the Virgin (August 15) brings households blessing and protection. Those who want to bind it correctly need to gather 77 different herbs!

During the Kirchweih, a fair held on the anniversary of the consecration of a church, everyone in the Danube region used to be given a Datsche and a Kirchweihknopf, two different types of pastries. Until the 1930s the Sichelhänke used to be celebrated, a scythe rite whereby every woman who cut with it had to weigh herself before and then after lunch – and the one who weighed the most afterwards was the winner.

In Allerseelen the priest still distributes Seelenbreze at christenings. These are small pretzels of the type that used to be eaten at wakes, or given to the poor.

The Nussmärtel, a noisy individual, still appears on the eve of November 11 in Northern Swabia, down to about the level of Gersthofen. South of that line, the equally nasty Klos appears on the eve of December 6, rewarding and punishing people respectively. The Klos actually existed in Nussmärtel territory for a while at the beginning of the 20th century, but was an invisible bearer of gifts. It was around that time that he was replaced in Swabia by the Christkind. The Barbarastrauss, or wreath of St. Barbara, decorated with sugar rings, was replaced by the Christmas tree in Northern Swabian Jura villages in around 1900.

The Klopferstag, originally on all four Thursdays in December, was made a fixture for the second Thursday in order to limit begging. In some villages even today, children knock a small wooden hammer against people's front doors, speak a rhyme to go with it, and are given apples, dried fruit and money in return. Sometimes they even get a baked pastry known as a Klosa.

Models of nativity scenes are an integral part of Swabia. They are generally placed in a part of the room known as the Herrgottsecke, and the figures are usually cut from clay or wood.

Today, the Sternsinger custom, similar to carol singing, seems to have become more a means of begging than collecting for charity. In the old days houses used to be »smoked out«, mostly with juniper twigs. Today all that remains of the rite is the incense accompanying the Epiphany custom.

At the beginning of the 21st century, Swabia is increasingly being influenced by fashionable rites from other parts of the world. Yet the faster fashions change, the more valuable the old, lasting traditions that have lent such colour and variety to the Swabian year.

Alois Sailer

Over 1600 children take part in the oldest children's festival in Bavaria, the Tänzelfest in Kaufbeuren. Photo: Verkehrsverein Kaufbeuren e.V.

Above and below: Trumpets and drums attract thousands of visitors to Memmingen each summer for the Fischertag festival. Crowds of people dressed in garlands and carrying blue-and-white flags pour through the streets around the small stream known as the Ach, cheered on by onlookers. This festival actually dates back to the 16th century: during late medieval times, when Memmingen flourished as an imperial city, its successful traders and craftsmen, weavers, dyers and blacksmiths used to line the banks of the Ach, a stream that was diverted through the town especially for them. To keep the stream clean it was emptied and cleaned once a year, and that meant that the trout had to be fished out first, by apprentices from the various local guilds. The fish were removed with special nets known as Bären, and once the water had been drained, the Schmotzer (stream-cleaners) could do their work. On the morning of the festival, the fishermen head for the Schrannenplatz, where the senior fisherman recites a few special phrases. Then at eight o'clock a small cannon is fired – the signal for all the fishermen to leap into the stream and do their best to catch the biggest trout. Once a trout has been caught, the women take over: they remove it from the net and put it in a special bucket. The fish is then weighed on scales set up in the market square, and the person who catches the heaviest one is the winner – the »Fisher King«.

Photos: Walter Dautzenberg

Churches & Monasteries

The two towers of Augsburg's cathedral tower mightily into the sky. They date from the Romanesque period. The west choir, in contrast, was converted in 1229 (see previous page). From left: »Samson and the Lion« in the wooden choir stalls of Augsburg cathedral, which date from 1495; the view from the font in the brightly-lit eastern choir of St. Ulrich; the »Simpertus Arch« behind the pulpit crowns the funeral chapel; the northern transept of St. Ulrich with a view of the magnificent rood screen; The Lutheran parish church of St. Anna in Augsburg, with a view of the chapel commissioned by Jakob Fugger, which contains his tomb and those of his brothers. Opposite page: view of the cloisters at St. Anna in Augsburg.

Swabia's historical development since the 13th century has made it a political patchwork. Historically, the map at the beginning of the 19th century was variegated to say the least. Over 150 independent territories were left behind when the old empire came to an end. By founding numerous monasteries and parishes during the 8th century, the bishops of Augsburg successfully established and expanded the influence of their diocese. Moreover, the many famous monasteries in the Swabian region competed with one another in order to strengthen their influence by establishing parishes in the region between the rivers Lech and Iller. Many parsonages and abbeys were lost during the Reformation and the Thirty Years' War, but this was remedied again by the church's strong religious and cultural commitment during the baroque era. In 1670 the bishopric of Augsburg had 110 monasteries, and 1,700 priests working in 866 parishes.

When the old empire came to an end, and the Final Recess of the Reichsdeputation was implemented at the beginning of the 19th century, the bishopric of Augsburg and the imperial lands occupied 57.5 percent of the region – the largest dominion in Swabia. Almost of half the population lived in church-administered territory. Eleven of the 13 imperial abbeys in Bavaria were situated in Swabia, and 100 years ago Bavaria had the densest network of parishes of any state.

The newly-Swabianised Bavarians had much baroque joie de vivre and cultural taste. At the end of the 18th century, the baroque style was omnipresent. The Enlightenment brought much renovation of church interiors, paving the way for secularization. During the 19th century, 17 foundations located inside and outside Swabia, 39 monasteries and innumerable monastic centres were dissolved – a loss that led to a serious artistic, cultural and educational impoverishment of the entire region. The cultural consequences of integrating Swabia into the kingdom of Bavaria were initially disastrous. It is nevertheless quite astounding how many early features of Christianity, especially the worship of St. Afra, managed to survive the stylistic revolutions of the past. The great monasteries were founded in the 11th and 12th centuries, mostly by the nobility, and a truly religious landscape was created. Augsburg and Swabia were forced to endure and survive all manner of religious-ideological conflicts. The Reformation and Counter-Reformation came to fruition in several towns and counties, and yet it remains a highlight of church history that the most important intellectual conflict culminated in the Confessio Augustana in Augsburg in 1530.

As the Reformation became firmly established in the free imperial cities of Swabia, the feeling of brotherhood and equality deriving from the Peace of Augsburg assumed a special significance. The ecumenical message of the Unaltered Augsburg Confession of 1530 is still a basis of hope today, and Augsburg remains a fine symbol of unity. Its ecumenical landmarks are the two churches of St. Ulrich: the magnificent Catholic basilica, and the Protestant one integrated into the same structure. The Catholic Church lost 24 monasteries and roughly 230 parishes as a result of the Reformation. Some of them were successfully regained during the Counter-Reformation, but people gradually became convinced that the Reformation was the right path to follow.

The Thirty Years' War was followed by a cultural blossoming in art, painting and architecture. Enormous monastery complexes were built, with magnificent churches: Kempten, Edelstetten, Irsee, Füssen and Ottobeuren, to name but a few. Every monastery or large church could easily afford magnificent new buildings, and the resulting baroque structures were often places of pilgrimage with a rich cultural heritage.

The University of Dillingen, converted into a lyceum in 1803/4, remained the spiritual centre. Integration into Bavaria was accompanied by the dissolution of the only university to be located on the Danube. This wrong has only very recently been righted – by the foundation of Augsburg University and its theological faculty.

The mighty churches and monasteries turned Swabia into one of the most fruitful cultural landscapes in Germany. For centuries, the work of numerous local artists and craftsmen was in great demand. Baroque and rococo decoration predominates, testifying to sheer wealth of artistic variety in this region. The religious orders, over 20 of them in all, were responsible for this cultural blossoming: they included the Benedictines and Cistercians as well as several mendicant orders. The Benedictine initiative alone resulted in 17 magnificent structures.

The collegiate church of St. Lorenz in Kempten was the first monumental monastery complex to be built in Germany after the Thirty Years' War, and marks the start of a development that would reach its magnificent conclusion a century later in Ottobeuren – one of the greatest architectural achievements of the 18th century. The buildings vary in size: some are centralized structures no larger than village churches, while others are either three-aisled High Medieval basilicas (such as St. Martin in Kaufbeuren), or Late Gothic structures (such as the Protestant church of St. George in Nördlingen).

The monastery church of Irsee (1699–1704), a late baroque structure with elaborate decoration. The most striking feature of the church is its pulpit, which is shaped like the prow of a ship (left). From above: The clear and simple lines of the western façade of the monastery church of Irsee. The steps of Irsee monastery, now an attractive congress and conference centre ever since its restoration by the Swabian district authorities. The banqueting hall in Irsee (Foto: Andreas Brücklmair) during an exhibition of artworks by the Augsburg painter Christofer Kochs.

The interiors of these buildings are just as magnificent as their exteriors. Major examples of fine church architecture include the Heilig Kreuz monastery in Donauwörth, the former monastery complex of St. Mang, the convent at Oberschönenfeld, the former Benedictine abbey of Irsee, and the pilgrimage church of Allerheiligen in Jettingen-Scheppach. Others are the former Benedictine monastery of St. Lorenz in Kempten, the pilgrimage church of Maria Steinbach, Lindau's parish church of Mariae Himmelfahrt, the Catholic parish church of Mariae Himmelfahrt in Obermedlingen, the monastery at Roggenburg, the former monastery complex at Thierhaupten, the chapel of St. Bartholomew in Aichach, the convent of Maria Königin der Engel in Bad Wörishofen, and the very attractively restored Frauenkirche in Günzburg.

Secularization greatly reduced the number of parishes and buildings, but the reorganisation also resulted in construction of new parishes that continued into the 20th century. In 1950, the diocese contained a total of 925 parishes, and many more were established as a result of past-war developments. Numerous independent cultural centres were set up in Swabia, sometimes in tiny villages, and the parish structure that resulted from this was very dense. The diocese of Augsburg and thus of Swabia is very different from the other Bavarian dioceses in this respect. From the architectural point of view this gave rise to a large number of parsonages, many of them listed buildings, and these are increasingly becoming a financial burden for the diocese. The historic monuments preservation society is inadequately funded, and it has been difficult to provide effective culture programmes with decentralised structures in many rural districts. When one reflects that large towns, in particular, still have sextons, chaplains, parsonages and tithe barns, the problem becomes far clearer, and more of a worldly than a religious one. The steady drop in the number of priests since the 1960s has meant that many of these buildings are uninhabited – indeed, almost half the 1,020 parishes in the diocese of Augsburg have no parish priest. As a rule, one clergyman is usually expected to look after several parishes at once. As a result of this dilemma, and despite financial assistance from the diocese of Augsburg, several fine rectories built by excellent architects have become disused and dilapidated. Over the past 25 years, 56 baroque parsonages and other church buildings have been demolished, despite their historical importance – this is a loss even greater than that suffered by such buildings after secularization.

The church and the parsonage remain the architectural and religious centre of most towns and villages, and are landmarks of historical and cultural importance. Complete or even partial demolition of these buildings often reflects a lack of historical awareness and a serious loss of local identity. Indeed, churches and parsonages are often the only historical buildings testifying to the past history of a town or village.

Above, top, and facing page: The Catholic Premonstratensian monastery church of Maria Himmelfahrt Roggenburg, the last work of the great Swabian architect Simpert Kraemer.
Above, centre: The former monastery church of St. Peter and Paul in Oberelchingen, converted in 1746 by architect Joseph Dossenberger. The interior is early neoclassical. View of the organ loft and elaborately decorated pulpit. Above, bottom: Wettenhausen monastery, a fortress-like structure that was once an Augustinian abbey.

Two centuries ago, Bavarian Swabia was a flourishing landscape full of monasteries. The secularization of 1802/3 had all the more devastating an effect on the region's economy and, above all, its culture. New research is making this ever clearer: Swabia is growing increasingly provincial. In his Handbook of Bavarian History (Vol 3, 2), Andreas Kraus writes: »When the great Swabian monasteries all over the countryside, all of them centres of learning and culture, were dissolved, Swabian intellectual life received a blow from which it would never recover.« Secularisation deprived Swabia of numerous cultural treasures, and the ensuing centralisation made the region increasingly desolate and provincial. Many monasteries were pulled down, while others were used by the state years later for entirely different purposes. These buildings include the magnificent abbeys of Niederschönenfeld or Kaisheim, both of which are prisons today, and also the monastery of St. Mang in Kempten which now houses the local law courts. Some important Swabian monasteries benefited from the partial repeal 20 years later by King Ludwig I, and his eagerness to repair at least some of the damage that secularization had caused; such fortunate establishments included the Benedictine abbey of Ottobeuren and the Cistercian abbey of Oberschönenfeld. Some other formerly magnificent centres were granted a new beginning during the 19th century, such as Ursberg, where Dominikus Ringeisen and the Congregation of St. Joseph set up a large institute for the disabled.

Other newly-founded monasteries or convents became schools; the former Augustinian abbey of Wettenhausen, for in-

Facing page: The Benedictine abbey of Ottobeuren in the Unterallgäu region. The magnificent interior of the basilica during one of the concerts that mark the high point of the cultural year. Several famous artists and architects contributed to this building, including Johann Michael Fischer, who completed the church in 1756. Above, 1 and 2: Ottobeuren Abbey is one of the highlights of South German baroque architecture.
Above, 3 and 4: The pilgrimage church of Maria Steinbach in the district of Unterallgäu, built from 1746 to 1754, and one of the greatest examples of the Bavarian-Swabian rococo style.

stance, or the Benedictine monastery of St. Stefan in Augsburg. Nevertheless, a whole series of huge and artistically important monastery complexes gradually fell into disrepair, and around 25 years ago, the formerly magnificent Swabian monasteries had been largely abandoned. Since that time, however, a great deal has been done to remedy the situation.

The district of Swabia decided to pay special attention to the restoration and partial reutilisation of its former monastery complexes, which had lost their former function as a result of secularization. In the European Preservation of Monuments Year of 1975, the former Benedictine abbey of Irsee was the first structure to be restored. Until then it had been used as a psychiatric hospital, and was seriously dilapidated. In 1974 the Swabian local authorities made the courageous decision to restore the complex to its former baroque splendour and turn it into an education and culture centre. This turned out to be very successful, and today Irsee is an adult education centre that is much in demand. The restoration of the abbey sparked off a series of similar renovation projects, and the sum of roughly 20 million marks that was spent – only very little of which came from state subsidies – seems quite small in retrospect.

Similar renovation work was carried out at the former monastery of Thierhaupten, Oberschönenfeld, Roggenburg monastery, the former Carthusian monastery in Buxheim, Obermedlingen, the Maria Königin der Engel monastery in Bad Wörishofen, the Heilig Kreuz monastery in Donauwörth, the former Capuchin monastery in Wemding, the monasteries in Memmingen and Mindelheim, and at the former convent in Edelstetten.

This restoration work has removed many of the scars inflicted by secularization, and now, 200 years on, the new cultural functions of these renovated buildings have given them a new lease of life. Each region has its own, typically local attributes with regard to economy or culture, and Swabia has profited greatly by injecting new life-blood into its ailing monasteries and convents. The decision to do so during the 1970s by the Swabian authorities was thus the right one. Sometimes one wonders whether or not the new functions assumed by the secularized monasteries, convents and churches, and their new and exciting future roles, have dispelled the devastating effects of secularization entirely. After all, a region once belittled as a mere province has now regained much of its former glory, and is ready to contribute fully to the culture and education of the 21st century. The decision to restore these structures to their former magnificence, and the efforts involved since that time, are characteristic features of a Swabian cultural policy that is firmly geared towards present and, most importantly, future considerations.

Georg Simnacher

Literature:
Fassl, Peter, »Bavarian Swabia«, second edition, Constance 1996, pp. 83 ff.;
Paula, Georg, »Swabia's Rich Cultural Landscape«, pp. 184 ff.

THE FUGGERS IN SWABIA

They began as poor weavers, and ended up running the most powerful city in Europe: the Fugger family. Their rise to ascendancy – economically, politically and socially – was quite unique. The weaving family became a family of merchants in Europe and overseas, and bankers for emperors, kings and even popes. In Augsburg, the former control centre of the Fugger trading empire, the Fuggers' former residential and business buildings at 36–38 Maximilianstrasse still stand as reminders of that time. The houses form a massive building complex, containing numerous large and small inner courtyards with Italian flair; the magnificent Renaissance tomb of Jakob Fugger in the Church of St. Anna, and the Fuggerei, founded in the early 16th century and still owned by the Fugger family today. It is the oldest housing estate in the world, and was built to give accommodation to married couples who had fallen on hard times through no fault of their own. The annual rent here is 0.88 Euros per apartment.

The Fuggers were also gifted land and property owners. They bought land strategically, as a long-term investment against unexpected economic crises. The land was then administered very carefully, and every attempt was made to retain it as a family possession that was not for sale.

The land acquired by Jakob Fugger the Rich (1459–1525) as a pledge from King Maximilian forms the basis of the Fuggers' territorial possessions. On July 27, 1507, for a loan of 50,000 guilders, the king made over the county and castle of Kirchberg on the Iller to Jakob Fugger and his heirs, together with the estates of Wullenstetten, Pfaffenhofen, Illerzell, Wiblingen, Weissenhorn, Buch and Marstetten. It was a large amount of territory, containing numerous castles, churches and villages, and even the entire town of Weissenhorn, which alongside Ulm was the centre of barchent weaving in Upper Germany. The Fuggers were accorded full sovereign rights, fiefs, jurisdiction and also hunting rights. The merchant had become an absolutist prince literally overnight. Nevertheless, Jakob Fugger faced strong hostility from the local nobility after he bought the county of Kirchberg, because they were unwilling to accept the citizen of Augsburg as their lord. Jakob Fugger was elevated to the ranks of the imperial nobility in 1511, and three years later became a count of the empire.

The important territorial acquisitions of Jakob Fugger's successor, his nephew Anton Fugger, included the estates of Nordendorf and Oberndorf on the large trading route that led to North Germany from Augsburg and Nuremberg. In August 1536, Anton Fugger was entrusted with the imperial city of Donauwörth; this allowed him to secure the most important Danube crossing for the emperor.

In April 1527 Anton Fugger had already purchased the estate of Gablingen, to the north of Augsburg, for 13,200 guilders. A little later, the village of Mickhausen to the southwest of the city was

Above: Jakob Fugger the Rich, as portrayed by Albrecht Dürer. Photo: Bavarian State Painting Collections.
Left: The chapel in the Church of St Anna in Augsburg, commissioned by Jakob Fugger in 1509, contains his tomb as well as those of his brothers Ulrich and Georg Fugger.

added. His negotiations for the purchase of the important trading town of Mindelheim were unsuccessful, however, even though he was prepared to pay more than 100,000 guilders for it. The reason for the rejection was the better offer for Mindelheim that was received from duke and elector Maximilian I of Bavaria, who was eager to strengthen his state against the Swabian free imperial cities.

The Fuggers' family castle is Babenhausen, beautifully situated in the valley of the River Günz. In 1538 Anton Fugger (1493–1560), also known as the »Merchant Prince«, bought the fiefdom from Duke Ulrich of Württemberg, and the land itself from the Knights of Rechberg in 1539. A mighty castle complex was built, and Anton Fugger and his wife Anna Rehlinger lie buried in the castle chapel.

Under the Fuggers, Babenhausen went through a period of economic and cultural prosperity until the Thirty Years' War, with its plague and famine, plunged everyone into deep despair. During the years following the French Revolution Babenhausen was loyal to emperor and empire, and this was honoured in the coat-of-arms that the Fugger counts still wear today. On August 1, 1803, Count Anselm Maria Fugger was promoted to the rank of imperial prince by the Emperor Franz II, and the estates of Babenhausen, Boos and Kettershausen collec-

Left, above, right: The inner courtyards of the Fugger buildings in Augsburg.

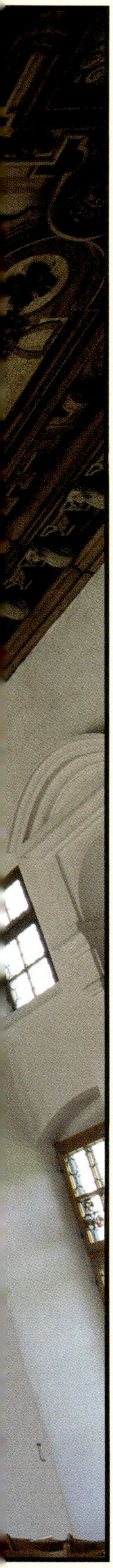

tively became the imperial principality of Babenhausen. Only a few years later, on July 12, 1806, the principality became a part of Bavaria.

In 1551 Anton Fugger acquired the estate of Kirchheim an der Mindel. When he died it fell to his son Hans Fugger (1531–1598), who also inherited Eppishausen, Mickhausen, Stettenfels, Glött, Schmiechen in Old Bavaria (and Türkenfeld and Adelshofen there too, later on), Dürrlauingen, Winterbach and Hafenhofen. He also purchased Reinhartshausen, Markt Dirlewang, Tiefenrieth, Dachserg, Pestenacker, Walleshausen and several more small counties. Hans Fugger was friendly with the Bavarian Duke Wilhelm V, an art lover. They used to »swap« such artists as Friedrich Sustris, Antonio Ponzano and Hubert Gerhard. In an era of courtly culture the Fuggers, too, wanted to hold court in magnificence; this is why their receptions in Kirchheim an der Mindel were just as stately as the ones at the court in Munich. The Fugger castles were not only very tastefully decorated with works of art but also had magnificent gardens and grounds. The women wore the finest materials and furs from all over the world, usually imported by the Fuggers themselves. At Kirchheim there were a vast number of servants, valuable horses, elegant hunting parties and also a court jester to entertain the illustrious guests. Hans Fugger spent 60,000 guilders a year on holding court in this fashion. Ever since the 17th century, the Fugger-owned territories have been the largest and most complex ever run by a single local family in Eastern Swabia. In the year 1658 the Fuggers owned over 60 villages, a small town and 43 districts. When one remembers the temporary ownership of the county of Mering, and the attempts made by Anton Fugger to secure the margravate of Burgau and even the palatine duchy of Neuburg on the Danube, it becomes very clear that the aim was to establish a loosely connected territorial and political union between the rivers Iller, Lech and Danube and Lake Constance (the county of Wasserburg was the southernmost Fugger possession). The name given to this area was for the future to decide – a margravate, or perhaps even a duchy. The Fugger lands survived integration into the kingdom of Bavaria at the beginning of the 19th century: the different dominions continued in the shape of state-recognized patrimonial courts, and the Fuggers themselves became landowners in the new kingdom. In 1913 Karl Ernst Ludwig Fugger von Glött (1859–1940) was elevated to the rank of a prince by King Ludwig III of Bavaria. Regardless of bankruptcies and wars, the Fuggers have always managed to preserve their social status as counts and princes.

Especially attractive Fugger sights in Bavaria include the family castles in Babenhausen and Kirchheim an der Mindel, because both are open to the public. The Fugger Museum was opened in 1955 in the oldest section of the castle in Babenhausen. The guided tour describes the heyday of the Fugger family in detail, the family history, and the influential role they played in the economic, political and social life of their time. Numerous valuable works of art and historical material give a good overview of developments during the past 400 years.

Above: Hans Fugger and his wife Elisabeth of Nothafft-Weissenstein (1531–1598). She was considered a great beauty in her day.

Facing page: The Cedar Hall in the Fugger castle in Kirchheim an der Mindel. Above left: The Fugger castle in Babenhausen.

The Fugger castle in Kirchheim an der Mindel, located on a gentle sandy slope above the valley of the river Flossach, is Kirchheim's most visible landmark because of the 70-metre-high tower, which dominates the entire valley. Hans Fugger (1531–1598) had a massive castle complex built from 1578 onwards, under the supervision of Augsburg master builder Jacob Eschey. The buildings are based on the Escorial in Spain – in other words, a unity of castle, church and monastery.

A memorable experience is a visit to the so-called Cedar Hall inside the castle – a massive banqueting hall 36 metres long and 12 metres wide. The ceiling, covering an area of 400 square metres, is one of the finest Renaissance works in Europe. It was created in 1585 by Wendel Dietrich. The Cedar Hall emanates what many Fuggers had become by the 16th century: patrons of the arts, especially music. This tradition is continued every year by the castle's owner, Princess Angela Fugger von Glött, with the summer concerts held in the Cedar Hall. The special thing about the Fuggers is not only that they created a massive trading empire of European as well as international importance, but that the noble family they founded has more than proven its greatness over the centuries.

Martha Schad

The Fuggerei in Augsburg – the oldest housing estate in the world. It was commissioned by Jakob Fugger and his brothers in 1516.

The Jewish synagogue in Augsburg, built between 1914 and 1917. Details of the magnificent interior and »Syrian style« dome.

Jewish Traces in Swabia

Jewish traces in Swabia? They don't immediately catch the eye. Some people never notice them at all. The cemeteries are frequently out of the way, surrounded by walls and sealed off. Synagogues are often only recognized by those who know something about them. But they are there, often used differently: converted into residential buildings, or used as schools or business centres. A search for Jewish traces is also a trip back through history. What was life like here for Jews? No-one knows how long Jews lived in the area covered by today's Germany; they may have arrived with the Romans. It was in Augsburg in 1212, however, that the first Jew, Josef of Augsburg, was mentioned in documents. A Jewish community seems to have quickly sprung up there with its own synagogue, ritual bath, rabbinate, school and dancing house. Names today provide something of a clue too: the street called Judenberg refers to its former inhabitants, and today's Rabenbad was once the rabbinate bath.

Jews lived in other cities apart from Augsburg too – mostly free imperial ones such as Donauwörth, Nördlingen and Memmingen. They were thus directly subordinate to the emperor. In exchange for a high fee, he supplied them with letters of protection. Since they were excluded from the guilds, moneylending was the only profession left to them – a job that incurred much ill will. After all, how can a creditor be popular? Reasons were continually sought and found to rid the towns of the Jews and wearisome debts. They were accused of desecrating the host, or made responsible for the plague – after all, their strict cleansing rites made them more resistant to disease than other citizens. During the plague year of 1348, for instance, 100 of Augsburg's 120 Jews were murdered. Letters and seals of protection from the emperor were no help at all. The Jews fared no better in other cities. In Nördlingen, for instance, a document reads: »All Jews in Nördlingen killed on St. Martha's Day 1348.« Eventually

Circumcision book

Jews were expelled entirely from all the cities. From 1438 to 1803, not a single Jew was allowed to live in Augsburg. In 1518 Donauwörth expelled its Jewish population too, and in 1599 the Emperor Ferdinand granted »freedom from Jews« to the town of Memmingen.

The Jews living out in the countryside started gaining in importance and leaving visible traces. At that time there was no consistent state territory. Pfersee, Hürben, Binswangen, Kriegshaber and Fischach belonged to the Austrian margravate of Burgau. Oettingen belonged to the princes of Oettingen, while other towns belonged to the prince-bishopric of Augsburg. Jews were allowed to settle in these areas because, after all, they made money. Sometimes almost half the population of these towns was Jewish. Kriegshaber, today a suburb of Augsburg, belonged to Vorderoesterreich, and a Jewish population was documented there from 1569 onwards. The synagogue on Ulmer Strasse is still in very good condition, but it now stands empty and needs a new function. The building can be easily recognised by the large Star of David above the door. The houses beside it, most of them shops, were all owned by Jews, and it is said that a corridor connected them with the synagogue so that the storekeepers could visit it without having to go out into the street first.

Today the name Am Judenhof in the middle of Fischach is a reminder of the Jews who once lived there. The former synagogue, today a lovingly restored and renovated residential building in which the Torah niche can still clearly be seen, lies directly beside the Catholic church. The Jews of Fischach contributed much to the development of the community. They were members of local associations and the voluntary fire brigade, and a plaque in the Jewish cemetery commemorates the men who fell in the First World War. When Jews were allowed back into the cities, the population here gradually dwindled as it did elsewhere. The last of Fischach's Jews were deported in 1942. A few years ago a monument was erected to their memory.

Three rural Jewish synagogues have been impressively renovated in the past few years: Ichenhausen, Binswangen and Hainsfarth. The least conspicuous of them is probably the one in Ichenhausen; ascribed to Joseph Dossenberger, it blends in well with the surrounding houses. If it had a tower it could even be taken for a church. Fortunately it escaped destruction on the infamous Kristallnacht because setting fire to it would have endangered the surrounding buildings. So at least the building was left standing; its interior was demolished. When Moritz Schmidt, the mayor at that time, wanted to renovate the synagogue – it was being used as a fire station at the time – he encountered great resistance, but did not give up. Today it has been restored to its former magnificence. The starry firmament on the roof is a reminder of God likening Abraham's seed to the stars of the heavens. The women's gallery has been preserved, and fine new windows have been built. The Jews are what is missing. The synagogue is not used for services today. The Torah shrine is only painted on, and an eternal flame no longer burns. The upper storey contains a permanent exhibition with numerous photographs, documents and even remains of the Torah shrine, providing a good impression of how the place used to look before the Holocaust. An important find was made in the attic: the Jews had hidden several cult objects and religious books. Seventy wimpel, or Torah binders, were also discovered here. What are they? A Jewish boy is circumcised when he is 10 days old. The nappy used to clothe him for this special rite was then cut into strips. Sewn together, these made a long band that was more or less artistically embroidered by their mothers with religious motifs: circumcision rites, bar mitzvahs, weddings. The band was then taken to the synagogue and used to bind the Torah scroll. This rite could only be found in Swabia, Franconia and Alsace. Torah binders can also be seen in the Jewish Museum in the synagogue in Augsburg.

Ichenhausen had a large and important Jewish community dating back to the year 1559. In the mid-19th century the town had 1,100 Jewish citizens, and was the second-largest Jewish community in Bavaria after Fürth.

Once a young girl asked me: »Is it true that all Jews are rich?« Her parents had apparently convinced her of it. Oh no, definitely not. Taxes were high, and the Jewish teacher Jakob Blum wrote that »the protected Jews of Ichenhausen had to bend over backwards to earn enough to stay out of debt, which would have meant losing their protected status«. Jewish associations for health care or for distributing firewood make it clear that there were many people in need. In addition, the number of Jewish households was strictly limited, and new ones were only possible if a member of an existing one died. Those who received no settlement permit had no fixed abode. Jewish beggars moved from one district to the

Torah scroll, Torah crown and Torah cloak, Jüdisches Kulturmuseum Augsburg-Schwaben.

Country synagogue in Ichenhausen.

Above, left: Moorish style country synagogue in Binswangen.
Above right: Country synagogue in Hainsfarth, near Oettingen.

next, and even though they received help from their fellow believers they always had to move on three days later. Several of them took the risky step of travelling to America, and sometimes managed to earn money and respect there as hard-working entrepreneurs. One famous example is Levi Strauss, born in Buttenheim, Franconia, the inventor of jeans; another is Michael Riess, who sent much of his money back to his home town of Wallerstein, continually visited it and actually died during one of those visits. His tomb can be found in the graveyard at Wallerstein.

The synagogue in Binswangen is quite a surprising sight, with its horseshoe-shaped windows and entrance portals, and its Gothic stepped gable crowned by the two commandment tablets and an iron serpent. If you enter the synagogue room itself, the decoration is a stunning red and blue, with striking palm-tree ornamentation on the capitals. This imposing, oriental-style building seems very out of place in a small farming village! Surely the Jews must have disqualified themselves in the small community by building such a magnificent place? The architecture was not their choice, however. King Ludwig I of Bavaria had defined certain characteristics that would enable people to notice at first glance whether a building was a school, church, town hall or synagogue, and had decided that the neo-Moorish style best suited the synagogues. And that is how the Jews of Binswangen were given this exotic place of worship.

During Kristallnacht, SA men forced a Jewish citizen of Binswangen to break down the door of the synagogue, and then proceeded to smash everything inside. From then on the building was used for all sorts of purposes. The pillars were torn out in 1967 and were one day offered for sale. At this point Josef Reissler intervened and saved the valuable pillars with the help of the office for the preservation of historic monuments. He was also the person who successfully persuaded the local authorities in Dillingen to renovate the synagogue.

The third renovated synagogue in Bavarian Swabia is in Hainsfarth, near Oettingen. Despite being rather inconspicuously located – almost in a »back yard« near the end of the village – it is also a magnificent building in neo-Moorish style, with a strikingly colourful interior. The Torah niche has not been plastered or painted over here, as in the other two synagogues. The red tiles were left here on purpose, like an open wound, in memory of what happened. The inscription above the entrance portal in golden Hebrew lettering is a line from Psalm 100: Enter his gates with thanksgiving, and his courts with praise; give thanks to him and praise his name! Beneath it, in Hebrew numerals, is the year of construction according to the Jewish calendar: the year 5620 after the Creation. The year of renovation is provided in Arabic numerals: 1996.

In Hainsfarth, too, the renovation of the synagogue sparked bitter resistance. Mayor Engelhardt received several fierce complaints and even death-threats. Even today, the synagogue is appreciated more by visitors than by the locals themselves. »Us Hainsfarth people don't go there, we don't,« a local once told me when I attended a concert in the building.

There are other synagogues in other places, but they now have different uses. The residential building in Oettingen that used to be a synagogue still has the window with the Star of David, and the one in Buttenwiesen is now a school. In Mönchsdeggingen the former mikvah, or Jewish ritual bath, is still well-preserved and is now a museum. The synagogue in Harburg, built in 1754, is located at the centre of the village on the bank of the Wörnitz – so the mikvah was once fed by the waters of the river. Despite a private initiative the building was not used for a cultural purpose but sold to a private buyer. The synagogue had a school and its own rabbinate, pointing to a large Jewish community. The cemetery on the Hühnerberg near the castle is the finest Jewish cemetery I know: the artistically designed gravestones bear loving inscriptions about the dead beneath them. The long texts in Hebrew – only the names sometimes appear in Latin script as well – are often shaped like an acrostic, i.e. the initial letters of the lines, read consecutively, form another word, usually the name of the deceased. Many tombstones also bear special symbols indicating the deceased's role in society. Praying hands mean

Jewish cemetery in Steinhart, near Oettingen.

that the dead person belonged to the kohanim, or priestly caste. A can is a reference to a Levite whose job was once to wash the priests in the temple. A knife indicates the circumciser, a book symbolises a Torah scholar. Other symbols, such as a half-moon, have no clear significance.

Our tour should end in Augsburg, where it began. Here, on Halderstrasse, is the only synagogue in Swabia that is still used for services. It was built between 1914 and 1917 by architects Heinrich Lömpel and Fritz Landauer when the old synagogue became too small. When the magnificent art nouveau building with its 29-metre-high dome was officially opened, the mayor at the time assured it »eternal protection.« This lasted until Kristallnacht on November 9th, 1938, when the interior was completely destroyed. No-one dared set the building alight because it was feared to be too close to a petrol dump. From then on the synagogue fell into disrepair, but it has now been resurrected. The renovation work was completed in 1985, thanks to the hard work and intervention of Senator Julius Spokojny.

A synagogue like this one says a great deal about the Jewish faith as well as about the people who celebrated it here. »Know in front of whom you are standing« warns an inscription in Hebrew at the front of the building, and the Eternal Light symbolises the presence of God. A flight of steps leads up to the Torah shrine on the eastern wall, which is covered by a valuable curtain. A synagogue contains no altar – it is not the temple, after all. There are no high priests and no sacrifice. Nothing remained of the Temple in Jerusalem after its destruction by the Romans in 70 AD. And yet the people scattered across the world knew that »their God went with them«, and that he was not tied to a temple. They still retained what was most important, as well as a »homeland to take with them« – the Torah. It contains writings about the chosen people of Israel, the promise to Abraham and freedom from the yoke of Egypt. It contains the commandments that God gave the Jews on Mount Sinai so that their life in freedom would succeed. Today the Torah – the five books of Moses – is still written by hand onto a long strip of parchment for religious services and then rolled up on two rollers. The Torah scroll is holy because it contains the name of God. And since it is all that remained of the temple service, it is lovingly adorned in a magnificent velvet cover, because the high priest also wore magnificent clothing. Stylised bells and pomegranates were attached to its hem, which is why silver bells are still attached to the roll on the Torah. The high priest wore a breastplate with 12 precious stones, representing the 12 tribes of Israel. The Torah scroll also has a sign attached to it, often artistically made of silver. For the service the Torah scroll is solemnly taken from the shrine and placed on a special table, and being summoned to read from it is a very special honour. During Simchat Torah, the festival of joy in the Torah, the scrolls are carried through the synagogue in a festive procession. The Torah is a »tree of life« to all who believe in it. The museum next door to the synagogue contains attractively decorated Torah scrolls such as these, along with ritual implements for festivals, pesach plates, chanukkah lights, scrolls, Torah wimpel and much more.

This community had to face change on a continual basis. The original furnishings make it clear that the congregation was liberal: the bima, or raised podium, from which the Torah was read is not at the centre of the room, as in most synagogues, but at one end, and this makes the whole place more reminiscent of a church. Above the Torah shrine there was once an organ, which was later sold to a church congregation near the Ammersee. When they wanted to return the organ to the synagogue after its restoration, the now rather orthodox community refused. Musical instruments are not allowed in synagogues as a sign of mourning for the destruction of the Temple. In past years the Jewish community here, whose numbers were dwindling, suddenly experienced a new lease of life with the influx of Jews from the former Soviet Union to Germany. Many of these new arrivals came to Augsburg. Alienated from their faith by circumstances, they are attending the synagogue again and learning about Jewish life. Circumcisions are taking place again, and weddings are again being held under the baldachin. Jewish life is returning. Mazel tow, good luck!

Gertrud Kellermann

Jewish cemetery in Hainsfarth, near Oettingen.

BASILICA SANCTI PAVLI

Swabians Portrayed

Swabians, runs an old saying, »have a hard head«. This is a slightly more subtle way of stating that the people who live between the Alps, the Ries, the Iller and the Lech are extremely stubborn – almost »pig-headed«, in fact. History from time immemorial has of course shown that the Swabian has not only used his head to push through his own insistencies but has certainly used it for the benefit of the rest of humanity as well. Whenever homo suevus starts thinking hard and long, there's always something brilliant at the other end. The German diminutive forms of Mächeler, Tüftler and Bäschtler are all regularly applied to Swabians, emphasizing their brilliantly inventive streak, their fondness for tricky, niggly problems and finicky jobs, and their ability to have strokes of genius at regular intervals. Swabia has continually brought forth talented researchers, inventors, discoverers, scientists and artists.

Another great talent Swabians possess is their astonishing caution with money. This kind of thrift would be called avarice anywhere else. In and around Augsburg this characteristic, combined with enormous diligence and a corresponding business ability, can certainly lead to an amassing of material values on a large scale, while out in the country districts it is more usually termed Interessiertheit or Hausigkeit – whereby the latter term should not be confused with Häuslichkeit, the word for domesticity. Hausig must mean a great deal to a Swabian, because the word aushausig translates as a love of extravagance.

Left: »The Basilica of San Paolo fuori le mura« panel by Hans Holbein the Elder, with scenes from the life of St. Paul.
Staatsgalerie Augsburg, on loan from the Bavarian State Painting Collection. Photo: Joachim Blauel, Artothek, Peissenberg.

One of the first Swabians ever to be portrayed was a woman. **St. Afra** who, legend has it, was a maid well-known in the town, apparently preferred to be burnt to death in the 3rd century AD rather than deny her Christian faith – a convincing example of a mind well and truly made up, which in this special case could also be interpreted as Swabian stubbornness.

A few centuries later, **Bishop Ulrich** (890–973) epitomised Swabian piety most impressively. He is considered one of the most important people of his age, and his name is inextricably associated with the Battle of Lechfeld (955) against Hungary. Far more important than his highly praised military abilities, which probably did not suit his personality that well, were his goodness, modesty, openness with ordinary people, social attitude and the example he set others as a human being – characteristics that won him a vast amount of respect even during his lifetime.

In Füssen is the tomb of a saint known as the »Apostle of the Allgäu«. Strictly speaking, **St. Magnus**, who lived from 699 to 772, is not a Swabian since he came from St. Gallen. He is however responsible for converting the people north of the Alps to Christianity and has thus been »borrowed«. The people of the Allgäu revere their »St. Mang« as a protector to this day, and treat the location of a holy footprint he left behind (jumping across the Lechschlucht Gorge near Füssen during an escape from his pagan pursuers) as a »sacred site«.

A namesake of the Allgäu missionary is **Albertus Magnus** (1193–1280) from Lauingen. As a philosopher, theologian, natural scientist and legal scholar, he can certainly be said to be the greatest Swabian of all time. A teacher, professor and universal genius, he was the person who »discovered« St. Thomas Aquinas, and his mind was centuries ahead of its time. His collection of medieval wisdom into 50 volumes formed the basis of a whole new age. »His Latin language is only a thin veil covering the intelligence and wisdom of a dyed-in-the-wool Swabian« – these words were written almost 800 years later by Joseph Bernhart, the theologian and philosopher born in Ursberg in 1881. Bernhart himself was greatly admired by Thomas Mann, who once confessed to never having been »capable of such power and such clarity of thought«.

On the subject of leading churchmen, one definitely must be mentioned: **Christoph von Schmid**, who has kept the happy Swabian attitude alive until today, 150 years after his death. He was a teacher, priest and author, and active and successful in Seeg, Nassenbeuren, Thannhausen and Augsburg. He achieved a kind of immortality with the famous German song »Ihr Kinderlein kommet ...«, which is probably the country's most-sung Christmas carol apart from Silent Night.

Another memorable Swabian was **Creszentia Höss**, a nun from Kaufbeuren. Her life was distinctive not only for deprivations and sufferings but also for the grandeur of an unshakable belief in God. Born over 300 years ago into a family of poor weavers, the young girl had to be very patient indeed to finally be accepted as a Franciscan nun even though her parents could not afford the dowry money. In the convent she suffered the bullying and blows of an unpleasant mother superior, and was even branded a witch until she became a highly-respected helper of the poor and sick. She was canonized only very recently, at the beginning of the 21st century.

During the 15th century, the life of another famous Swabian woman took a tragic turn. **Agnes Bernauer**, the daughter of a barber from Augsburg and apparently a very beautiful, turned the head of Albrecht III, son of Duke Ernst of Bavaria so much that he secretly married her, despite having been forbidden to do so by his parents. The Bavarian duke started an evil intrigue against his unwanted daughter-in-law, and she ended up being accused of witchcraft and drowned in the Danube. This drama, one of the most moving of the Middle Ages, was thus of Swabian origin, and was welcome material for the stage.

Women in Swabia are certainly not lacking in attractiveness. This was also documented by

Leopold Mozart's Violinschule. Photo: Augsburg State Library.

Wolfgang Amadeus Mozart, the musical genius from the Swabian family of the same name and son of the Augsburg Kapellmeister **Leopold Mozart**, who had an open, lively and sometimes rather naughty exchange of correspondence with his female cousin »Bäsle« in Augsburg.

By the way, classical music fans worldwide will be interested to know that the Mozart voice of all time came from Swabia. **Irmgard Seefried**, a teacher's daughter from Köngetried near Mindelheim, received her training at the Augsburg music conservatory, married the famous violinist Wolfgang Schneiderhan, debuted under Herbert von Karajan in Aachen and remained a member of the Vienna State Opera until her death in 1988. Fans of light entertainment, in contrast, idolised the Augsburg-born actor and singer Gerd Höllerich, known by his artist name of **Roy Black**, and continue to mourn him ten years after his tragic death.

Jakob Fugger, the son of a Swabian weaver, was the embodiment of efficiency in both business and finance. During the 15th century he was considered the world's wealthiest man, and became known as »Jakob Fugger the Rich«. He financed all the rulers of his time, especially the emperor Maximilian, and his money and influence allowed him to influence world politics: he prevented the French king Francois from being crowned emperor in place of the Habsburg Karl V. His great fondness for art as well as ordinary people is reflected in

numerous important works of art and buildings, especially the so-called »Fuggerei«, a settlement for the poor and needy which today is the world's oldest housing estate. Jakob Fugger's patronage enabled many of his fellow Swabian contemporaries, including the painters **Hans Burgkmair** and the two

Holbeins to achieve world popularity. Burgkmair was allowed to illustrate the Emperor Maximilian's prayer book – together with Albrecht Dürer, Lukas Cranach, Albrecht Altdorfer and other great artists of that time. Late Gothic church painting reached its peak in the 15th century under Hans **Holbein the Elder**, while his son **Hans Holbein the Younger** perfected his father's skill at portraiture, and became not only the most important but also the highest-paid German painter of the Renaissance.

Elias Holl, the mastermind behind Augsburg's magnificent Town Hall and other supreme architectural achievements of his home city, died in bitter poverty in 1646. Petty-minded town councillors had decided that the master builder's »false faith« – he was Lutheran – was enough of an excuse to dismiss him.

The sheer brilliance of a Swabian mind was revealed by the Jesuit priest **Christoph Scheiner** from Markt Wald in Central Swabia, who became one of the most important natural scientists of the 17th century alongside Kepler and Galileo. He invented the pantograph, an instrument for copying a geometric shape to a larger or smaller scale, and he was also the first to construct elliptical compasses. With Galileo and other astronomers he discovered sunspots, and this led to a fierce argument about who had spotted the spots first. Demonstrating typically Swabian modesty and reserve, Scheiner published his later observations and descriptions under a pseudonym.

In contrast to the legend about the Seven Swabians, the region has also produced numerous brave and valiant people. One such was **Georg von Frundsberg** (1473–1528) from Mindelheim. He was commander-in-chief of the armed forces of his time, and as »Father of the Lansquenets« he was employed by the emperors Maximilian and Karl V.

A very different kind of bravery was displayed by his fellow Swabians who risked and sometimes lost their lives during the mid-20th century in the fight against national socialism, one of them being the officer **Claus Graf Schenk von Stauffenberg**, born in Jettingen Castle near Günzburg, who was executed in Berlin in 1944 after the assassination attempt on Hitler failed. The Meitingen priest **Max Josef Metzger** also died for resisting the evil regime – he was guillotined.

Left: Elias Holl was Augsburg's master builder from 1602–1631. This 1711 copperplate engraving by Heinrich Jonas Ostertag shows the Ludwigsplatz with Town Hall, Perlach Tower and Augustus Fountain, and a view north up the Karolinenstrasse.
Right: Portrait of Rudolf Diesel with his famous diesel engine. Photo: Historisches Archiv MAN AG, Augsburg.

Pondering and fiddling were always at the root of the Swabian urge to research and invent. Not surprising, therefore, that the Diesel engine was invented in Augsburg. Even though **Rudolf Diesel** was the son of Swabian parents, he was born in Paris, where his father was trying to keep the family going as a small-time manufacturer. Since then his invention has always been associated with his name – the same cannot be said of **Sebastian Wilhelm Valentin Bauer** (1822–1875) from Dillingen. The designer of the first submersible submarine has been forgotten – apart from memorabilia and documentation in his home town.

Then again, another Swabian »invention« will probably bear the name of its maker for ever: the special water cure developed by **Sebastian Kneipp** (1821–1897). It was a salutary »drastic cure« by the priests from the seminary in Stefansried near Ottobeuren that inspired Kneipp to develop one of the most successful natural therapies, transforming the village of Wörishofen into a world-renowned spa and becoming increasingly successful right up to the present day. The »water doctor's« patients during his lifetime included popes, royal highnesses and millionaires. Kneipp »put a damper« on his customers' all-too-high expectations of attaining eternal life from his hot-and-cold footbaths and cold compresses with his famous statement: »They all want to grow old, but no-one seems interested in dying!«

When a Swabian attracts others' attention with his entrepreneurial spirit, his fellow Swabians talk of a person with Unternimm. **Hermann Köhl** had a great supply of it. Born in Neu-Ulm, he crossed the Atlantic from east to west one year after Lindbergh had done so in the opposite direction, and made aviation history together with his co-pilot Freiherr von Hünenfeld and the Irish aviator Fitzmaurice.

Another courageous and entrepreneurial Swabian was the Munich-born **Anderl Heckmair** from Oberstdorf, the first man to scale the notorious northern face of the Eiger in 1938. And the reason that the Allgäu is Germany's cheese paradise today was the work of **Carl Hirnbein**, from the Western Allgäu, who made a huge success out of the diary industry there during the mid-19th century.

Below: Bertolt Brecht's notebook »Memories of Marie A«. Photo: Bertolt Brecht Archiv, Berlin.
Below (and facing page): Bertolt Brecht at the Augsburg photographer Konrad Ressler. Photos: Fotomuseum in the Munich Stadtmuseum.

As was the case with Elias Holl, the people of Augsburg had difficulties with another of their great sons 300 years later. In this case it was definitely a mutual antipathy: the world-famous dramatist, author and director **Bertolt Brecht**, who happily retained his Lech-Swabian accent in his German and even in his English, was held in deep contempt by his home city after he converted to communism and emigrated from Germany to escape the Nazis. Ever since his death, however, Augsburg has been happy to make peace with him and boast of him as one of its own. Brecht was certainly not the only Swabian to attract attention as a writer; other gifted authors from this part of the world include **Hans Magnus Enzensberger** from Kaufbeuren, a much-praised essayist and the winner of the German Academy's Georg Büchner Prize. Another equally successful author is Martin Walser from Lake Constance, who recently won the Peace Prize from the German book trade. **Ludwig Ganghofer**, **Peter Dörfler** and the Mindelheim-based **Arthur Maximilian Miller** are all more than worthy of mention, too. Swabia has also produced great composers and conductors: **Eugen Jochum**, for instance, one of Germany's greatest music scholars and the founder of Augsburg's famous

Singschule. Or **Werner Egk** from Auchsesheim near Donauwörth, whose operas »The Magic Violin« and »Peer Gynt«, and Faust ballet »Abraxas« are world-famous.

If the Swabians are so industrious, intelligent and successful, surely there must be a few Nobel Prize winners among their ranks? Indeed there are: **Johann Deisenhofer** from Zusamaltheim, son of a farmer, professor at the Howard Hughes Medical Institute in Texas, was warded the Nobel Prize for biochemistry in 1988, together with Robert Huber and Hartmut Michel. The researchers had discovered a way of looking inside a biological »photocell«, and of determining the three-dimensional structure of a photosynthetic reaction centre.

Another Swabian Nobel Prize winner was Dr. Erwin Neher, a biophysicist from Buchloe, who won the Nobel Prize for medicine and physiology jointly with Heidelberg doctor and biophysicist Bert Sakmann in 1991. Dr. **Erwin Neher** is a graduate of the Maristenschule in Mindelheim.

Swabians have also excelled in sports: how many people know, for instance, that the internationally successful professional golfer **Bernhard Langer** comes from the little village of Anhausen near Augsburg? Or that Augsburg has also produced **»Gold-Heidi« Schmid**, who won the ladies' fencing Olympics in Rome, or **Elisabeth Micheler-Jones**, world canoeing champion in 1992? There is also **Helmut Haller**, the footballer worshipped internationally for his »golden legs« – his typically Swabian »hard head« produced a great number of goals.

Any attempt to collect together a representative group of Swabians who have done much to spread the fame of their home region far and wide would be incomplete without a mention of the **wooden puppets from the Augsburger Puppenkiste**, whose popularity on television has done a great deal to promote Swabian hard-headedness internationally!

Winfried Striebel

CULTURAL CREATIVITY

Greenfly in Greenland? Ski-jumping in Kinshasa? Culture in Swabia? In this gentle landscape, famous cultural events on the international level are conspicuous by their absence. There are plenty of green hills, but no Bayreuth. No Documenta, no Cannes-like glamour, no Metropolitan Opera. The world-famous museums are not on the banks of the Günz or the Kammel, but the successors of royal collections in metropolises like Paris, London or Madrid. Or Bilbao. And even fringe events in the culture scene are established elsewhere. For jazz, people make the pilgrimage to Burghausen, and for contemporary music to Donaueschingen. Culture in Swabia?

There are, of course, the »Romantic Road« and the »Swabian Baroque Route«, leading from one magnificent church to the next. There are majestic monasteries all over the place, and the green hills of Swabia are adorned with fortresses and castles. The centres of the former free imperial cities have a sleepy magic all their own, and also – in the case of Augsburg – several important monuments to industrial architecture as well. There are various traces of Roman settlement, from Kempten to the Ries. And from the great god of Altenstadt and the bronze portal of Augsburg Cathedral to the statues on the altar of St. George in Nördlingen, the residence in Kempten and the sublime basilica of Ottobeuren, this land definitely breathes culture and reveals constant traces of cultural creativity – but it is a creativity of the past. Gone are the days when the goldsmiths among Augsburg's population outnumbered its bakers, when there were dozens of copper engravers and publishers, when Johann Georg Bergmüller ran the Imperial Academy of Art and when people made frequent mention of »Augsburg taste« as a moving force in rococo decoration. Much later there was Bertolt Brecht, who gained a world reputation as a poet and dramatist – elsewhere. Culture in Swabia? From a global point of view, no chance. Using a rather smaller yardstick, however, it is certainly possible to find much that is charming and appealing in the cultural scene. One just has to look, and it's easy to miss a great deal in the process.

The impressive return of several Bertolt Brecht »classics« in Augsburg's Municipal Theatre: here, a scene from »The Threepenny Opera« in 2003. Photo: Lioba Schöneck.

Tradition and progress on the Kennedyplatz: Matschinsky-Denninghoff's stainless-steel sculpture »Easter« has been standing outside the Augsburg Municipal Theatre since 1986.

A draw for the public since 1929: the Augsburg Freilichtbühne open-air stage at the Rotes Tor (Red Gate) lends a Mediterranean feel to summer evenings.

The Swabian Theatre Scene. Theatre in Swabia is actually quite easy to find. It flourishes from Lindau to the historic municipal theatre in Weissenhorn, and all the way to Donauwörth. The traditional Swabian Landestheater, based in Memmingen (where plays were being put on as early as the days following World War One!), does guest performances in over 40 towns and districts. With at least seven new productions each year, there are also several premieres – such as the Heavy Metal opera »Clytemnestra or the Flight of the Atreides«, which even caused a stir abroad. The programme is usually rather more staid, even though varied. In 2003, for instance, the municipal theatre in Kempten had old and new classics in its programme ranging from Calderon and Molière to Sartre and Dürrenmatt, and the civic halls all over Swabia are frequently used for all kinds of touring productions. Sometimes they are worth visiting for their atmosphere alone – the magnificent Kurhaus Theatre in Göggingen, for instance, built in 1885 by Jean Keller and now reawakened from its enchanted sleep by excellent renovation work. Here the productions and the venue blend together superbly for unforgettable experiences. Theatre in Swabia is not only the fixed ensembles in Memmingen and Augsburg, however, but also the very numerous theatre associations and enthusiastic amateur companies, some of which can be very good indeed – the Romanist-Theater from Augsburg University, for example, which has now become something of a cult institution. The Passion Play Association of Waal has fulfilled tradition since 1960 with its own 800-seat theatre and a performance that harks to the plague year of 1626. The combination of folk costumes and intelligent theatre is a real eye-opener for contemporary audiences.

Augsburg Municipal Theatre. Augsburg is definitely the centre of Swabian theatrical life. It has a long tradition: the »Meistersinger-Stadel« was the town theatre in 1665. New operas performed in the building constructed in 1777 included Mozart's »Don Giovanni« and works by Wagner and Verdi (1853–58), while the new theatre built in 1877 featured several German first performances, including one of Ibsen's »Ghosts«. In 1919 the theatre established itself as a municipal enterprise, and after the structure destroyed in World War II was rebuilt in 1956, the first performance – very suitably for Augsburg – was Mozart's »Marriage of Figaro«. Augsburg still has a high culture budget, despite regular moaning from those who have to sponsor it – industry, the city, and the »Friends of the Municipal Theatre Association« – and provides regular performances of operas, operettas, plays and ballet.

For a long time the city's Städtische Bühnen (municipal theatre) was considered a springboard for young talent. »Conductor prodigies« who began their careers here include Wolfgang Sawallisch, Heinz Wallberg, Istvan Kertesz or Bruno Weil. The internationally celebrated conductor Eugen Jochum was born in Babenhausen. TV star Harald Schmidt, Hans Korte, tenors Chris Merritt, Douglas Nasrawi and Bavarian Kammersänger Ulrich Ress all began their careers on stage in Augsburg. Artistic ups and downs and tight cultural budgets are a continual problem, and a new playhouse is also needed. Recently an astonished press has begun writing about a »renaissance of Augsburg theatre«.

Visitor numbers for the 2000/2001 season were higher than for any other theatre in Germany, and

The Kurhaus Theatre in Göggingen: a masterpiece of illusionist art, and since 1996 back in business as a theatre.

Puppet magic: an exotic scene from »Cabaret« (2003) by the Augsburger Puppenkiste. Photo: Elmar Herr

Augsburger Puppenkiste

Oehmichens Marionetten Theater

celebrated actors from all over the country are being attracted to Augsburg. Theatre manager and artistic director Ulrich Peters and senior director Holger Schultze both believe that a town like Augsburg needs stimulation. No boring programmes, therefore, but a lot of first performances, modern productions, new actors, better service (providing »insights« into the productions), and a love of experimentation. While the large theatre with its 936 seats offers attractive classics, the Komödie next door is now home to thriving experimental drama. Young playwrights and directors enjoy using the Forum, which has an innovative freshness that even the theatre metropolis of Munich is beginning to notice. In April 2003 Schultze and the 21 members of his ensemble teamed up with some guest actors and successfully tackled Botho Strauss's play »The Fool and his Wife This Evening in Pancomedia«, which requires a cast of 100 people and until then seemed to be the exclusive preserve of larger houses.

The Augsburg Philharmonic Orchestra provides ten symphony concerts and two youth concerts every year; the dance ensemble presents two ballet evenings with its own productions; and the tradition of the Freilichtbühne open-air stage, which started in 1929, still continues: streams of visitors arrive from all over the place clutching woolly blankets and umbrellas, peering worriedly at the summer skies. With such a great atmosphere, even the legendary August Everding from Munich could not resist an invitation to put on a production here.

The success of theatrical life in Augsburg is also reflected by almost 20 ballet schools, the children's and youth theatres, and cabaret and variety in the »Mühle« and also the »Kulturhaus Abraxas« with its intimate auditorium, which has been a success ever since it started in 1995 on the site of a former barracks. Augsburg is also famous for its young musicians. The municipal theatre is an essential part of artistic life in the city, not only because of its direct cultural role but also because of the synergy effects on culture in the entire region, also in collaboration with the city's university, design academy and music conservatory. For this reason, the city intends to do as many financial gymnastics as it can to keep all the activities going. It is quite clear from the streams of visitors that the people of Augsburg love their theatre – even those who continue to regularly attend subscription series in Munich.

Popular puppet theatre. And of course they also love their very own »Augsburger Puppenkiste«, the only cultural product of the city to enjoy nationwide popularity in Germany. The success story of this puppet theatre, founded after the war by Walter Oehmichen, is now being continued by the third generation of the Marschall family. The television programmes starring the puppets – »Urmel aus dem Eis«, »Jim Knopf« or »Lukas, der Lokomotivführer«, to name but a few – have now acquired cult status for young and old alike, at home and abroad. The Augsburger Puppenkiste began its rise to fame with the live television programme »Peter and the Wolf« on January 21, 1953. Now, fifty years on, there have been 785 TV productions. Aficionados will soon be able to continue appreciating the familiar programme in the newly-renovated theatre plus puppet museum in the Heilig-Geist Spital; there will be legends and fairy tales for the young, and operas, plays and cabaret for adults.

The Swabian Youth Symphony Orchestra – a good example of Swabia's powerful support for music.

Chamber concerts in Schloss Leitheim, once an insider tip, are unforgettable experiences – and are discreetly sponsored by the castle owner!

With such a famous puppet theatre, it comes as no surprise that Augsburg also hosts the international »Puppenspieltage«, or »Puppet Play Festival«. This quickly established itself, largely because of the high quality of the performances, plus a great deal of innovation, inventive genius, different types of puppets and highly imaginative set designs. It started 16 years ago and is now a fixed event in the city's cultural calendar. Another puppet theatre in Swabia is the »Moussong«, which now performs in the Kulturhaus Abraxas – and in Lindau there is even an established »Marionette Opera«.

Music in Swabia. The fact that Mozart came from this part of the world doesn't really need to be emphasised – the Swabians are definitely musical. All you need to do is listen: there is music in every village. In fact, The Allgäu and Swabia Music Association lists 663 music clubs. Karl Kling, long-time president of the oldest German brass-band music association, did a great deal to promote this state of affairs. Almost every parish has a brass band, Nördlingen has a town orchestra, and some churches have their own choirs. The Augsburg »Domsingknaben« choirboys are of course in a class unto themselves, but churches have contributed a great deal towards keeping music popular. There are numerous concerts during the »Füssen Organ Summer«, for instance, featuring historic church organs; the »Monastery music in the Allgäu«, with organ concerts at 4pm each Saturday in Ottobeuren between February and November; the »Roggenburg Summer«, and also all the churches inside Augsburg itself. In addition there are numerous choirs, from the Philharmonic Choir and Swabian Choral Association to the ensemble »Chorfeo« which only has 16 members. The latter, run by the gifted Wayne Wegener, won the German choral competition with a performance of »vocal jazz«. Everyone sings and plays in Bavarian Swabia, and if you take a walk during a summer evening you just need to follow the sounds – there is always a choir or orchestra rehearsal somewhere.

Much is being done to help and promote gifted young musicians. Immenstadt, to give just one example among many, has a music school with 18 teachers and 684 pupils. On the district level there is the Swabian Youth Symphony Orchestra, while the Bavarian Music Academy in Marktoberdorf has its own regional Jazz Youth Orchestra. Krumbach has a vocational academy for music. The Swabians are so keen on music that it is good to know that the Leopold Mozart Conservatory in Augsburg has now teamed up with the one in Nuremberg to form a double music conservatory, because the standard of musicianship is now even higher. The Leopold Mozart violin-playing competition has an excellent reputation worldwide, and is attended by entrants from all over the world.

No wonder, then, that the cultural events calendar is brimming with concerts and music festivals throughout Swabia. And there is no shortage of visitors. Classical music in the Lindau Municipal Theatre and the Protestant Hospital, lieder evenings in the baroque hall of the Vöhlin castle in Illertissen, concerts in the Oettingen Residenz (with partly free admission to young people under 16), the Kunstfrühling festival in Wörishofen run by Justus Frantz, the Kneipp music festival run by Martin Haselböck, and the concerts in the Fürstensaal in Füssen in which classical mixes with modern and also jazz, are

»Klang und Raum« (Sound and Space) combine in the choir of the church at Irsee Monastery to create a memorable experience.

The King Ludwig Theatre, near Füssen, houses the musical based on the life story of the »Mad King« of Bavaria, »Yearning for Paradise«.
Photo: Brinkhoff/Mögenburg

just a few of the events on offer in this part of the country. Most concert series can look back on 50 years or more of tradition, and architecturally they often have a direct link with the time the music was first written – baroque halls and rococo churches, for instance. Sound and venue thus blend into a very special experience. Such places include Leitheim Castle, which has staged around 20 concerts every year since 1959, the highly atmospheric »Kleiner Goldener Saal« in Augsburg, or the grandiose majesty of the monastery church of Ottobeuren, where just a few bars from the famous 66-register Riepp organ are enough to transport audiences straight to heaven.

The »Ottobeuren Concerts« – run by Wolfgang Sawallisch, the famous Beethoven and Bruckner conductor – are a highlight of Swabian musical life. Others include the »Festival Summer in the Wies«, with performances in the Welfenmünster in Steingaden and St. Michael in Altenstadt under oratorio conductor Franz Brannekemper, and the »Klang und Raum« (Sound and Space) music festival at Irsee Monastery, under the artistic direction of Bruno Weil with his Tafelmusik orchestra from Canada and the Tölz Boys' Choir, held on the first weekend in September each year. The Augsburg Mozart Summer is also well worth a visit.

Luckily, musical life in Swabia is not the exclusive preserve of the big city. Neuburg (mentioned here because of its influence on Northern Swabia) not only offers baroque concerts in historical locations together with historical dress by candlelight, but also the »International Neuburg Easter Academy for Ancient Music and the Fine Arts«, in cooperation with the University of Regensburg. During the »Summer Academy« there is also a chance to study piano improvisation with Professor Herbert Wiedemann from the Berlin Academy of the Arts, who was born in Lindenberg in the Allgäu. The Irsee summer academy »Kunst leben« has close ties with institutes of further education and also lecturers, especially from Augsburg University. The whole summer is rounded off by the art festival »Kunstnacht Irsee«, which is definitely worth a visit.

Musical Swabia is not just limited to classical music, of course. Since April 2000 fans of musicals have been making the pilgrimage to Füssen to see the musical based on the life of Mad King Ludwig of Bavaria, in a theatre by the Forggensee that was especially built for the purpose. There are 400 performances of the musical each year. Producer Stephan Barbarino is convinced that the nostalgia project will soon start to break even.

International rock and pop concerts take place on the Burghalde open-air stage in Füssen, in Memmingen, and in Augsburg. From the Jazz Club in Lindau to Wolfgang Lackerschmid's »Traumraum« in Augsburg (an insider tip), famous international performers are a regular fixture. Bass player Christian Stock has started his own »Augsburg Jazz Summer« festival, jazz has also been long established in Neuburg – and the Kempten »Jazz Spring« festival is now one of the largest in Germany.

Jazz players are naturally not only interpreters but also composers of their own works. Wolfgang Lackerschmid has composed his own theatre music for the municipal theatre. It is no surprise to musically enthusiastic Swabians that contemporary mu-

Much in demand on the international scene: the Augsburger Wolfgang Lackerschmid (on the vibraphone) and his »Traumraum«. Photo: Helmut Ölschlegel

The big-band sound at the Kemptener Jazz Spring festival with the Cambodunum Big Band and their leader Dieter Müller. Photo: Kleinkunstverein Klecks

sic is still being composed after Werner Egk (1901–83). On New Year's Eve 1999, the Ulrich Vespers by Josef Hauber were performed in the Augsburg basilica of St. Ulrich and Afra. Swabia is not the place for very avant-garde music, however: Gerhard Haugg, a native of Augsburg, only managed to have his »Ufopera« first performed in the tiny gallery »Kulturesk«. His »Mobile Phone Symphony« premiered at the third European Festival of Chamber Music and Music Theatre in Düsseldorf, and his »Internet Opera« was first performed by the North Rhine-Westphalia Landesorchester. The sounds of Swabia are thus reaching beyond its borders.

Reading and Writing. Literature in Swabia is more a matter of matter of communication and presentation, since there has been little produced since the days of Brecht. There is a great deal of literature down at Lake Constance, of course, from Droste to Martin Walser. Otherwise it is hard to come up with more than a few names for the 20th century: Alexander von Bernus (1880–1965) from Aeschach near Lindau, Hedwig Lachmann or Oskar Schürer from Augsburg, whose lyric production fell silent after 1919, or perhaps, embarrassingly, the fanatical Hitler supporter Richard Euringer, who won the National Literature Prize in 1933.

Literature in Swabia? One can of course point to the world-famous intellectual and literary heavyweight Hans Magnus Enzensberger; he refuses to be called »Swabian«, however, despite the fact that he was born in Kaufbeuren in 1929. Facility with words and political commitment were attested to this winner of the Büchner Prize (1963) from an early age and even resulted in comparisons with Heine, even the form of his literary output: poems, essays and commentaries. His life revolves around European cultural history and world literature rather than the Allgäu.

Winfried G. Sebald, born in Wertach in 1944, didn't stay in Swabia either. He worked as a lecturer in Norwich since 1970, and developed an unusual and captivating prose style in tales and novels such as »Austerlitz« and »Die Ringe des Saturn«. His rhythmical sentence structures turn descriptions into a matter of inclination and discretion. Sebald was awarded the Mörike Prize, the Heinrich Böll and the Heinrich Heine Prize. The great author was fatally injured in a car accident in the year 2001. Swabian novelists worthy of mention include Georg Klein with »Barbar Rosa« and »Libidissi«, and Gerhard Köpf who today lives in Duisburg and wrote »Innerfern«, »Piranesis Traum« and also »Die Strecke«, filmed under the title of »Wallers letzter Gang«.

Literature in Swabia? There are of course authors who come from Swabia such as Wolfgang Bächler or even Rainer Werner Fassbinder (1945–82) from Bad Wörishofen. Fassbinder the dramatist was eclipsed by his outstanding success in »New German Cinema«. His most successful play, »Die Bremer Freiheit« (1972), has however been staged around 70 times.

Other authors living in Swabia include Franz Dobler, Wolfgang Kunz, Erich Pfefferlen, Susanne Seitz or the Augsburg cultural adviser Eva Leipprand. In 1996 »Keine laute Provinz« was published, an anthology of contemporary authors from Swabia that was commendable even though rather brief in places. Anyone intending to write a literary history of Swabia could

An attentive audience for »Sarastros stille Liebe« by Attila Csampai, read by the author at the Rieger + Kranzfelder. One of Augsburg's most traditional bookshops, with a 270-year history, it is located in the historic Fugger Houses on Maximilianstrasse.

Literature in the beer garden:
Emil Steinberger reading in the »Drei Königinnen« beer garden in Augsburg.

also include literati such as the Büchner Prize winner Heinz Piontek (1976) or Erhard Kästner as guests in the region, and perhaps all those who gave guest speeches or could be caught passing through as well. Because the local heroes of the literary scene are just that – local.

Literature is of course produced in Swabia. There is an excellent historical, art-historical and scientific literary output – all the brilliant, linguistically inventive essays by Helmut Koopmann, for instance, on literature of the 18th to 20th centuries. And apart from local literary prizes there is also the Bavarian Swabia Prize for Literature from the Arthur Maximilian Miller Foundation of the district of Swabia.

Yet the most important literary achievement in Swabia remains the »Andere Bibliothek« (»Other Library«) edition from the bookstore and publishing house Greno in Nördlingen – in other words, a contribution toward dissemination of literature. In an amazing 218 volumes, the publisher, Hans Magnus Enzensberger, has saved a huge treasure trove of literary gems from oblivion, or introduced them to the German reading public for the very first time. Dissemination is thus Swabia's own special contribution to the literature of the present. Readings and literary events are refreshingly popular in Augsburg, and have become established items on the cultural agenda. Events such as »Literature in the Beer Garden« (Kurt Idrizovic) have ploughed up the earth, readings by guest poets at the university (including Gunter Künert) have acted as fertilizer, and the seeds are now growing in committed bookshops with ambitious selections – not only large ones such as »Pustet« but also traditional stores like Rieger and Kranzfelder on Augsburg's Maximilianstrasse. Seven bookshops have now joined forces to become the »Augsburg Literature Team«.

Augsburg (formerly the printing capital of the empire) devotes a vast amount of lectures, readings and theatre performances to a single author during the first three months of each year as part of the »Augsburg City Literature Project« – from Heine, Kafka, Schiller and Brecht to Zweig, Hesse and Mann. Each time there are cultural interrelationships right across the city, from the university to the cinema, the cabaret to the adult education centre, the bookstores to the artists' union and the municipal theatre to the vocational academy, all of them creating literary connections. The literature project has now been in existence for 10 years and has attracted all kinds of famous names to the city of Brecht: (from A to Z) Ilse Aichinger, Wolf Biermann, Robert Gernhardt, Nina Hagen, Walter Jens, Hellmuth Karasek, Adolf Muschg, Will Quadflieg, Jan Philipp Reemtsma, Marcel Reich-Ranicki, Hanna Schygulla, Gabriele Wohmann, Hans Wollschläger and Gerhard Zwerenz. So literature in Swabia does exist – when it's invited here.

The Fine Arts. Swabia's geographical position has had a negative effect on its fine arts scene. Far away from the brisk activity in the Ruhr region or in Berlin, and jammed between the academic cities of Stuttgart and Munich as traditional art centres, Swabia has assumed the characteristics of a talent supplier of secondary importance. Munich has around 400 galleries, 16 of which are represented at Art Cologne; Stuttgart has eight; and Swabia does not have a single one

A masterly line and fine-quality paint in the Georg Bernhard Studio. Photo: Traudl Bühler

Contemporary art in a baroque frame. The Kißlegg Kulturförderkreis presents work by Augsburg painter Christopher Kochs with the exhibition »Gegenwelt« in the Neues Schloss. Photo: Andreas Brücklmair

causing any kind of furore, not even on a national level. Nevertheless there is a good gallery scene from Lindau (Galerie Holbein, Galerie Doris Wullkopf) to Augsburg in which artists famed beyond the local region are represented – it's just that they are represented on a small scale.

After the death of Hans-Jörg Rehklau, exhibitors such as Konrad Oberländer, the Galerie Noah, Kulturesk or the Ecke Galerie are thus keeping in touch with the big world of art outside by switching emphases. The Galerie Neuendorf in Memmingen is also worthy of note. For a long time the people of Augsburg were gladdened by the famous »Nationale der Zeichnung« (Konrad Oberländer and Dr. Gode Krämer) and, at ten-yearly intervals, by the »Sculptors in Germany« exhibition (initiated by the Augsburg Art Association under Dr. Stefan Vogel). In the renovated Holbein House, with much-improved presentation potential, the Augsburg Art Association exhibits contemporary art of a high standard. The Höhmann House on Maximilianstrasse is being used by Dr. Thomas Elsen, curator for contemporary art in the Municipal Art Collection, to provide a refreshingly varied programme without making any concessions to »public taste«.

The Kunsthaus in Kaufbeuren also presents ambitious programmes. Graphics by Baselitz or installations by Fabricio Plessi have alternated with thematic exhibitions on witty and provocative themes, and these have not only attracted numerous visitors from outside but also – thanks to exemplary organisation – large crowds of children and young people. Since 1985 the town of Wertingen has made a name for itself in the scene with its annual, Bavaria-wide »Art in the Castle« exhibition series, while garnering itself a remarkable collection of contemporary art for the town's Municipal Gallery. Since July 2001, Marktoberdorf has had an architecturally attractive »Künstlerhaus« to go with its Eastern Allgäu Art Exhibition each October, though the brick-wall structure inside, destined for contemporary art, poses several problems for small-format pictures. And last but not least, the »Kunstkreis Aichach« under the competent management of Andreas Stucken is also more than worthy of mention.

Since 1999, using famous names such as Miró, Dalí, Hundertwasser or Ernst Fuchs, a regional group of promoters has been quite successful in attracting crowds to Augsburg. The organisers are not bothered by the fact that experts have been arguing about the quality of the exhibits, or that the concept comes across as a little stale. Papers from outside Augsburg regard the exhibitions as »provincial«, but the local newspaper has been effusive in its praise. And – »it gets the crowds in, dunnit«?

The emphasis is on presentation and communication of art in this sector too, and that provides an idea of the situation facing the scene at present. There are numerous artists of course, with open days for their studios, between Augsburg and the Allgäu. Ever since the 1970s there have been symposia in Lindau, Gundelfingen, Aichach, Mertingen, Wangen and Wertingen, as well as the »Westallgäuer Kunsttage« in Lindenberg and Weiler, plus sculpture paths and routes, collective exhibitions and individual presentations by the Professional Association of Fine

Painting as realization of reality by means of colour: Harry Meyer, »Hills in the Allgäu«, oil on canvas, 70 x 40 cm, 2001.

Artists. Various art prizes are awarded by districts, towns, savings banks and also artists' associations such as the traditional »Die Ecke« in Augsburg. Admittedly, the last Swabian winners of the »Villa Romana« prize were sculptor Willi Weiner from Zusmarshausen and Stephan Huber from Lichtenberg – in 1985 and 1986. Neither lives in Swabia any longer. Weiner's studio is in Stuttgart, and Huber moved to Munich; the latter has achieved international significance (including documenta 8 and the Venice Biennale of 1999). Günther Forg from Füssen has also turned his back on Swabia, though Christian Hörl (Ruderatshofen), Bernd Rummert (Konradshofen), Johann Schickinger (Höchstädt), Alf Setzer (Betzigau) or Stefan Stoll (Bachern) all at least promise to continue the sculpting tradition of such great names as Theo Bechteler (1903–93). Augsburg-born Alfred Görig is also a sculptor famed beyond the borders of Swabia.

Even though Augsburg was one of the first cities to host exhibitions of modern paintings, as early as 1945 in fact, Swabia has never become a centre of contemporary art. Karl Kunz remains an exception here during the post-war era, as does Heinz Butz from Dillingen (born 1925), who taught at the Munich Academy from 1967 onwards, and also the gifted, colour-sensitive Georg Bernhard from the technical high school in Augsburg. He succeeded in getting artistically important university teachers to come to the city, including Beuys pupil Jonas Hafner, or Joachim Palm. Regional painters who have also gained a reputation beyond their local area include Eugen Müller, Herbert Dlouhy (Wertingen), Horst Heilmann (Kempten), Karl S. Büchner (born in Lindau), Peter Zeiler (Irsee) or the colour sensualist Norbert Kiening from Diedorf, who is still a member of the younger generation. As exponents of the outsider art, Armin Rienecker and especially Wolfgang Hueber (Kaufbeuren) have made names for themselves. The rather short-lived Augsburg artist group »Freibank« caused a stir internationally in 1990 with the »prix jeune peinture étrangère« in the Grand Palais, Paris. Peter Lochmüller and the conceptually independent Gerhard Fauser have also established themselves as individual artists. Harry Meyer (who has won several prizes, most recently the Helen Abbott prize, Berlin and New York) and Christopher Kochs (also a prizewinner, he stayed in Sydney on a scholarship during 2001) have both made the leap to important galleries and the international art market. And this despite the fact that they live in Augsburg, a city that made contemporary art headlines recently with its noisy repudiation of sculptor Markus Lüpertz's »Aphrodite« statue. Max Kaminski has recently opened a studio in Augsburg too.

Museums. Swabia lacks a museum on the level of the »New Museum Nuremberg« (opened in 2000) or the »Pinakothek der Moderne« (opened in 2002), or anything even remotely close to it. Nevertheless, it does now have the »Kunstmuseum Walter«, which presents the collection of Augsburg construction entrepreneur Ignaz Walter inside the wonderful industrial building known as the »Glaspalast«, or Glass Palace. There are some big names among the 700 or so exhibits: Baselitz, Immendorf, Lüpertz, Penck, Polke, Rainer and Richter. In the glass collection special mention must be made of Egidio Constantini, but there is also work by Arp, Braque,

The Ries Crater Museum in Nördlingen. This geological museum dealing with the unique Ries landscape was set up by the town of Nördlingen and is administered by the State Natural Science Collections of Bavaria. It was originally started as part of the Rieser Kulturtage festival.

The Roman past, close up: adventure archaeology in Kempten. The Cambodunum archaeology park was opened in 1983, and there are also special guided tours for children.

Chagall and Picasso. The objective here was a »high-quality collection that provides a systematic and comprehensive overview of post-war artistic creativity«. The exhibition that has resulted is very individual.

Swabia's museum landscape is dominated by history museums, starting with the numerous folk museums devoted to local history. These include archaeology and Roman traces in Kempten and Mindelheim, the Roman Museum in Augsburg, the »Riesenkrater Museum« in Nördlingen, and the »Forum of Swabian History« in Höchstätt Castle, opened in 2002 after 15 years of renovation work. The most successful of Swabia's rural museums is south-west of Augsburg: the Swabian folk museum of Oberschönenfeld, surrounded by a magnificent Cistercian convent. The history of work and technology is presented by farm museums (Illerbeuren, Diepholz and Maihingen), the textile museum in Mindelheim (Sandtner Foundation) the Swabian Tower-Clock Museum, which contains the largest and oldest collection in Germany, the charming Hat Museum in Lindenberg, and the Bavarian Railway Museum in Nördlingen. The planned Textile Museum in Augsburg promises to be a real highlight, complete with excellent pattern books of European standard, while the Swabian Architecture Museum in Augsburg's Thelott Quarter is in a class of its own.

As far as art museums are concerned, the State Gallery ones in Augsburg and Füssen are excellent, as is the Late Gothic art in the »Alpenländische Galerie« in Kempten and also the well-stocked Municipal Art Collection in Augsburg with its German Baroque Gallery. The niches at the museum contain several nice surprises: Füssen, for instance, has work by Franz von Pocci in its Municipal Gallery, and Donauwörth has a Käthe Kruse Doll Museum. It's certainly worth taking a stroll round Swabia's museums, even though more important establishments with international reputations are not exactly situated on the banks of Günz or the Kammel.

Cultural Niches. Apart from the traditional institutions of high culture such as the museum, the concert hall and the theatre, cultural niches established themselves long ago and developed other forms. This refers to individual sectors such as film – after all, the days when Augsburg was the location of premieres with the likes of Romy Schneider are long gone.

Today the Independent Film Festival and the Augsburg Short Film Festival receive international attention. So does cabaret (Augsburg Cabaret Festival) and also new forms of cultural life such as the »Kresslesmühle« scene, which grew up from the alternative youth culture, with its enterprising boss Hansi Ruile and the international festival »La Piazza«. Large-scale events for today's youth culture with public rock and pop performances, such as Augsburg's »X-Large«, have unfortunately been axed for financial reasons. There are some interesting special offers for children, however, such as the Kinderkulturtage in Memmingen, or the Kinderfilmtage (Children's Film Festival) in Augsburg. In general there seems to be a gradual shift from high culture (which may tend to come across as too snobbish) towards festival-style, action-based events.

Inside the Roman Museum in Augsburg (formerly the Dominican church of St. Magdalena, built between 1513 and 1515, baroquefied 1716-24, and converted into the museum in 1966).

The German Baroque Gallery in a suitable setting: the numerous rooms inside the Schaezlerpalais in Augsburg (1765–70) contain such works of art as the »Veduta of Piazza San Marco in Venice« by Canaletto, painted in around 1735.

Alternative Events. There is hardly a town, monastery or church in Swabia that does not provide some kind of music festival in the summer. There is so much on offer that Swabian culture fans find it hard to choose between events taking place from Neuburg, Irsee and Schongau to Roggenburg, Memmingen (Memminger Meile) and Füssen. In addition there are numerous different types of festival ranging from jazz to puppetry, from brass band music (January 31, Buchloe) to museum nights, and from literature projects to baroque music. The »Rieser Kulturtage« festival takes place every two years and has attracted around 100,000 visitors each time, with almost 2000 individual events. Special emphasis is placed on integration of the disabled and on youth participation. Some of these initiatives have lasted, such as the Ries Crater Museum, the Friends of the Hainsfarth Synagogue, the International Rosetti Society, and also several adventure trails in the Ries.

Future Opportunities. While culture in some places seems to have been reduced to the level of the VHS videotape, communities with traditional »high culture« programmes are increasingly astonished at the change towards an event culture. Bavarian Swabia is under-supplied culturally in relation to Bavaria as a whole. When Munich and Nuremberg used the proceeds from privatization to further stock up their already-full museums, Swabia was left empty-handed. Munich also has an unfair advantage when it comes to state subsidies for cultural projects.

Trying to remedy this situation is out of the question at present – not merely because the state coffers are empty but also because highly-subsidized institutions are gradually being called into question. A lack of fixed ensembles and enormous theatres, of massive art galleries and of established events with a world reputation does not necessarily mean a lack of culture. In Swabia it merely flourishes on a smaller scale. The specific future opportunities for culture here lie first of all in the special aspects of the place: Ottobeuren is just as unique as Leitheim, Irsee or Lindau. An exquisite location is just the place to create exquisite cultural attractions. Swabia's secondary role geographically, its large flat expanses and its historical lack of unity all still pose problems, but here regional networking (as in the Ries) or the use of synergy effects by multipurpose events (Irsee) or festivals can work real miracles. The universities and high schools will soon be further involved in Augsburg or Irsee, just as the internationally established Psychotherapy Weeks in April and the Nobel Prize winner conference have become part of the calendar in Lindau.

Swabia thus has an individual cultural landscape of its own with exquisite locations, local niche cultures and cultural networking to festivals and events. Initiatives such as Augsburg's application to become the cultural capital of Europe might be considered rather laughable by those from outside, but the very idea itself is enough to stimulate local cultural activities and strengthen the readiness to cooperate, so that a strong cultural network can be created from numerous links. And that may be the seed of future opportunity. There may be no greenfly in Greenland and no interest in ski-jumping in Kinshasa – but there really is culture in Swabia.

Andreas Link

Photographers

Harald Hollo

Born in Stuttgart in 1948, he grew up in Augsburg and is married with three children. He qualified as a typesetter, and did his master's examination in 1972. This was followed by stays abroad, in Zurich and Vienna. He then studied graphic design at the Werkkunstschule in Augsburg, and went on to teach printing technology at the Graphic Academy in Munich. He spent several years as a lecturer at the College of Design in Augsburg and on the examining board of the Chamber of Industry and Commerce. From 1986 onward he has been the managing partner of Satz und Grafik Partner, Augsburg, and has published numerous art books together with Professor Georg Bernhard, Andreas Bindl, Agnes Keil, Christofer Kochs, Harry Meyer, Eugen Müller and Konrad Oberländer, to name but a few. His last published book was in 2000: »Augsburg – Town Views«.

Helmut Schreiber

Born in Eltville, Rheingau. Secondary education in Landsberg/Lech, then at the College of Photography in Munich. He worked as a photographer for advertising agencies in Altenkunstadt and Stuttgart, and had his own studio in Florence, Italy for six years. He then took his master's examination in photography in his parents' home town of Augsburg. He taught for six years at the College of Design in Augsburg, spending six months in Portugal and making several trips to Italy (Rome, Aeolian Islands). His work is regularly exhibited in Augsburg and Florence. He is happily married and now lives in Augsburg.

Published by

Satz und Grafik Partner GmbH, © 2003
Spicherer Straße 1, 86157 Augsburg
Tel. 08 21/3 43 23-0, Fax 08 21/3 43 23-33
E-Mail: hollo@satz-und-grafik-partner.de

Project and Production

Harald Hollo,
Satz und Grafik Partner GmbH, Augsburg

Setting and Lithography

Satz und Grafik Partner GmbH, Augsburg

Title Page

Foto Neuschwanstein: Getty Images/Merten

Printed by

Kessler Verlagsdruckerei, Bobingen

Paper

UPM finesse — UPM-Kymmene Group
UPM Finesse 300, 150 g/m²

Printed in Germany

MAN Roland
Druckmaschinen AG
Augsburg

Authors

Prof. Dr. Hans Frei

Born in Augsburg in 1937. After leaving school he studied geography, history and German in Munich, then passed his high school teaching diploma. After gaining his doctorate he was scientific adviser at the Geographical Institute of Munich University. From 1970 he worked as a country custodian for Swabia focusing on preservation of monuments, folk tradition and cultural landscapes, and especially on the upkeep and maintenance of museums. The combination of preserving traditions and engaging in scientific research work led to him founding and running the museums of Oberschönenfeld, Maihingen and Naichen. He has published and written numerous works on the subject of Swabia and its people. He is a lecturer and honorary professor of cultural geography and regional studies at the universities of Augsburg and Munich.

Gertrud Kellermann

Gertrud Kellermann was born in Augsburg, and grew up there. After passing her A-levels in Erlangen she decided not to study teaching, and married a priest. This marked the start of a long period of hard work and commitment in several parishes. After years in Landshut and later in Upper Franconia, she then returned to Swabia. Her commitment soon spread beyond the borders of her own region, and she has been working with great enthusiasm towards further education for women. Several trips to Israel interested her deeply in Judaism and the Old Testament, and she now assists the managing board of the Association for Christian-Jewish Cooperation – while finding the time to look after her seven grandchildren.

Dr. Rudolf Köppler

Born in Berlin in 1936, he studied law and political science in Berlin and in Erlangen. He then gained his doctorate with a dissertation on the constitutional status of political parties. A senior government councillor in 1970, he chose to live in Swabia after having been elected mayor of the town of Günzburg on five occasions up to 2002. A regional councillor, district councillor, lecturer and examiner of young law students, he publishes books and essays on legal science, and also writes novels, poems, satirical articles and short stories.

Eva Leipprand

Born in Erlangen in 1947, she grew up in Munich. She studied English and history in Würzburg and Munich, spending a year in England in between. Marriage took her to Stuttgart, where she spent 17 years as a high school teacher and mother of two. Since 1989 she has lived and worked in Augsburg as a freelance author. She worked with various citizens' action groups, and chaired the Forum Augsburg from 1994 to 2002. From 1996 to 2002 she was a city councillor, and since 2002 she has been a cultural representative and deputy mayor of Augsburg.

Andreas Link

Born in Dachau in 1949. The moral catastrophe linked with his birthplace made him sensitive to two subjects in particular: theology and art. He studied Protestant theology, theatre science and jazz in Neuendettelsau, Tübingen, Munich and Erlangen. He then worked for the local community in Selb and Fürth. From 1984 onwards he was a religion teacher at polytechnic schools in Augsburg, and ran a gallery of contemporary art on the side. He has published books and articles on teaching religion, town history, the relationship between art and the church, theory of art, and individual artists.

Manuela Mayr

Born in 1954, in Waldshut on the Upper Rhine. Spent a wonderful childhood in Southern Baden, strongly influenced by her Bavarian grandparents. Ever since leaving school she has worked as a journalist. Straight after her A-levels she spent time in Berlin and Venice. She is now professionally »stranded« with the Augsburger Allgemeine newspaper, where she works as an editor for the »Bavaria and the World« section. She settled down in Kühbach, Bavaria. With her husband, a native of the Eastern Allgäu, she enjoys country life there on an old farm that was mentioned in documents even before the Thirty Years' War.

Susanne Lorenz-Munkler

Born 1961 in Immenstadt, she grew up in Kempten and has always been an enthusiastic »Allgäuerin«. After passing her school leaving examinations in Kempten she worked on a voluntary basis for the Allgäuer Zeitung newspaper. In 1984 she moved to Augsburg, where she spent seven years working for the Augsburger Allgemeine. After the birth of her first child she returned to the Allgäu. Today her family of four lives in Krugzell, a village north of Kempten, where the author works and writes articles for newspapers and magazines on a freelance basis. Her hobbies include reading, mountaineering, skiing and riding – often with her husband and children.

Eduard Ohm

Born in the Bavarian frontier town of Neu-Ulm in 1945, he still lives there today. He studied law in Munich, and also did some art and theatre criticism – then became theatre and art critic for the Neu-Ulmer Zeitung. Until 1975 he edited the arts pages of the Augsburger Allgemeine. From 1977 he was a primary school teacher, and a headmaster from 1987. He is still active in the regional studies sector. He co-published the »Ulmanach«, an Ulm anthology that also includes several sorties into Baden-Württemberg territory. He has written books about his home town of Neu-Ulm, e.g. »Neu-Ulm – Augenblicke aus dem Leben einer Stadt«, as well as about the local district («Bei uns daheim«). He has also written a whole series of articles in catalogues for local artists.

Erich Pawlu

Retired senior high school teacher and publisher. Born in 1934 in Frankstadt, he took his A-levels at the secondary school in Ingolstadt before going on to do German studies, history and geography at Munich University. From 1959 to 1996 he was a teacher at the Johann Michael Sailer secondary school in Dillingen. He has written innumerable satires, first published in the Süddeutsche Zeitung, the Neue Zürcher Zeitung, Die Welt and the Frankfurter Rundschau, as well as radio sketches, schools radio programmes, reports, and articles for arts sections. He is also the author of school textbooks, volumes of prose, poetry and satire. He has been awarded several literary prizes, including the N. Lenau Prize for poetry. He was also given the Achievement Award Medal, and has also been honoured by his home town of Dillingen by being awarded the Bürgerbrief.

Alois Sailer

Born in Lauterbach in 1936, he is a Catholic from an old Swabian family. He writes about agriculture, works towards preservation of rural regions on a local basis, and lives with his wife Martha on the property he inherited in Lauterbach. After two semesters of agricultural studies and the study of German literature he worked for newspapers, magazines, radio and television. He has written numerous plays, such as the »Waal Passion Play« from 1969 to 1970. His literary work includes his study of dialect »Schwäbische Trilogie«, the tales in the »Wasserbirnenbaum« and the German poetry volume entitled »Späte Amsellieder«. Despite his rejection of literary competitions he has received several awards, including the Federal Service Cross.

Dr. Martha Schad

Dr. Martha Schad was born in Munich in 1939 and went to school in Augsburg. After studying at Cambridge and the Sorbonne she got married, and was soon the happy mother of son Albert and daughter Annette. She returned to Augsburg in 1975 and spent many years doing guided tours of the city, while studying history and history of art at Augsburg University. After gaining her doctorate she developed her interest in the »feminine side« of history. Her publications include »Die Frauen des Hauses Fugger«, »Die Königinnen Bayerns«, »Kaiserin Elisabeth und Ihre Töchter«, »Cosima Wagner und Ludwig II von Bayern«, »Mathilde Wesendonck«, »Frauen gegen Hitler« and »Hitlers Spionin«. Her »Augsburg City Guide« (available in English) was published quite recently, as was a book on the Bavarian King Ludwig II. From 2000 she has been an honorary country custodian of the City of Augsburg and is chairwoman of the Augsburg branch of the Richard Wagner Society.

Thomas Scherer

Born in Munich in 1958 to a mother from Augsburg, he is very familiar with the different mentalities of the two cities. Thomas Scherer inherited his love of journalism and writing from his Munich father; his love of changing places quickly was something he discovered himself. After working in Berlin and the Bayerischer Rundfunk's Bonn studio he became local head of the Bayerischer Rundfunk in Munich. In 2000 he was given the opportunity of setting up a new BR radio correspondent's office in Lindau, and now, as he says himself, he lives and works »where others go for their holidays«. Thomas Scherer is married and has two daughters, whose vitality makes writing difficult and life very pleasant.

Freddy Schissler

Born in Frankfurt on the Main in 1962, married with one child; he went to school in Villingen-Schwenningen in the Black Forest, then studied social sciences in Konstanz and Stuttgart. It was a job as a trainee with the Allgäuer Zeitung and the Augsburger Allgemeine that brought him to the Allgäu. This was followed by almost five years as an editor of the Memminger Zeitung. He then switched to the Sports section of the Allgäuer Zeitung as a deputy head of department, and from 1995 he was active as a freelance journalist for various newspapers (including the Allgäuer Zeitung, Augsburger Allgemeine, Stuttgarter Zeitung, Sonntag aktuell, taz, Südkurier, Schwäbische Zeitung). In 1996 he returned to the Allgäuer Zeitung, where he is now head of the culture section, and is thus still closely involved with the town of Memmingen and the surrounding region.

Dr. Georg Simnacher

Born the son of a ropemaker in Ziemetshausen in 1932, he studied in Munich and Erlangen, where he gained his doctorate in 1958. As a young law student he quickly rose in the ranks as a government official in Munich before switching to politics in the mid-1960s. In 1967 he became Bavaria's youngest regional councillor in Günzburg, and in 1974 was elected president of the Swabian area assembly. In 2003 Simnacher will be the oldest serving assembly president, and he is especially active in the social and health sectors. He contributed greatly to psychiatric hospitals being developed into modern clinics, and to decentralisation of psychiatry in the region. His commitment to the preservation of historical monuments has led to much restoration and renovation work (e.g. Irsee Monastery, Thierhaupten, Kurhaus Theatre). He has also written numerous historical studies.

Dr. Wilfried Sponsel

Born in 1955 in Heidenheim/Brenz, he grew up in Nördlingen. He studied Protestant theology, philosophy, education science, history and psychology in Tübingen. He then studied to become a civil servant, and gained a qualification as a secondary school teacher. In 1987 he was employed as an archivist in the Oettingen archives in Wallerstein and Harburg, simultaneously attending the archive school in the Bavarian State Archives. In 1991 he gained his doctorate at Augsburg University with Professor Dr. Pankraz Fried, professor for Bavarian and Swabian regional history. Since 1991 he has been an archivist – and country custodian – of the town of Nördlingen. He is a member of the Swabian Research Association and also works for several cultural institutions and associations.

Winfried Striebel

A self-confessed Swabian with a very hard head, born in 1932 in Schlingen (Lower Allgäu). His parents were teachers, with great initiative and interest in their local region. They soon introduced him to numerous Swabian guests such as Sebastian Kneipp, Georg von Frundsberg, Peter Dörfler, Joseph Bernhardt, Eugen Jochum, Arthur Maximilian Miller, Irmgard Seefried and many more. He attended secondary school in Kempten, then trained as an editor in Mindelheim. Journalism then took him to Bad Wörishofen, Marktoberdorf, Kaufbeuren and Augsburg, where he was a reporter, head of department and then editor-in-chief. Since 1997 he has been a freelance journalist. His motto for work and life is to »keep both feet on the ground all the time and stay close to people«.

Dr. Andrea Zinnecker

Born in 1963 in Marktoberdorf in the Eastern Allgäu. Then went to Würzburg and Augsburg for folklore studies, German studies and art history. This was followed by studies in Florence. In 1995 she gained her doctorate in folklore studies with a paper on the reception during the Nazi era of Wilhelm Heinrich von Riehl, the founder of German folklore studies. From 1984 onwards she was employed as an editor in the mountaineering department of the Bayerischer Rundfunk, and since 1993 she has been the station's Allgäu correspondent as well as a prolific author of culture- and history-related features.

Town/town centre worth a visit
Church worth a visit
Monastery/Convent
Castle, fortress
Ruined castle or fortress
Synagogue, former synagogue
Airport
Romantic Road
Upper Swabian Baroque Route
Swabian Spa Route
0 5 10 15 20 km
Hessen
Thüringen
Sachsen
Schwaben
BAYERN
Baden-Württemberg
Augsburg
München
© Bezirk Schwaben, Augsburg
Nördlingen
Oettingen
Wemding
Donauwörth
Harburg
Lkr. Donau-Ries
Lkr. Dillingen
Dillingen
Lauingen
Gundelfingen
Wertingen
Meitingen
Lkr. Aichach-Friedberg
Aichach
Gersthofen
Neusäß
AUGSBURG
Friedberg
Stadtbergen
Lkr. Augsburg
Bobingen
Königsbrunn
Schwabmünchen
Günzburg
Lkr. Günzburg
Leipheim
Burgau
Ichenhausen
Krumbach
Neu-Ulm
Lkr. Neu-Ulm
Senden
Weißenhorn
Vöhringen
Illertissen
Mindelheim
Türkheim
Buchloe
Bad Wörishofen
Memmingen
Lkr. Unterallgäu
Ottobeuren
Bad Grönenbach
Kaufbeuren
Marktoberdorf
Lkr. Ostallgäu
Kempten
Füssen
Lindenberg
Lkr. Lindau
Lindau
Oberstaufen
Immenstadt
Sonthofen
Lkr. Oberallgäu
Oberstdorf
Bodensee
Ulm
Aalen
Heidenheim
Ellwangen
Bopfingen
INGOLSTADT
Eichstätt
Treuchtlingen
Weißenburg
Neuburg
Dachau
MÜNCHEN
Fürstenfeldbruck
Landsberg
Starnberg
Weilheim
Schongau
Garmisch-Partenkirchen
Biberach
Ravensburg
Weingarten
Leutkirch
Bad Waldsee
Bad Wurzach
Isny
Wangen
Bregenz
Dornbirn
Feldkirch
Reutte
Innsbruck
BADEN-WÜRTTEMBERG
ÖSTERREICH